GOVERNMENT PROCEDURES AND OPERATIONS

Additional books in this series can be found on Nova's website under the Series tab.

Additional e-books in this series can be found on Nova's website under the e-book tab.

GOVERNMENT PROCEDURES AND OPERATIONS

MILITARY WHISTLEBLOWER REPRISAL INVESTIGATIONS

OVERSIGHT ISSUES AND INSPECTOR GENERAL GUIDANCE

JESSE L. PORTER
EDITOR

nova publishers
New York

Library of Congress Cataloging-in-Publication Data

ISBN: 978-1-63483-938-9

Published by Nova Science Publishers, Inc. † New York

CONTENTS

PREFACE

Whistleblowers play an important role in safeguarding the federal government against waste, fraud, and abuse. However, reporting wrongdoing outside the chain of command conflicts with military guidance, which emphasizes using the chain of command to resolve problems. Whistleblowers who make a report risk reprisal from their unit, such as being demoted or separated. DOD's Office of Inspector General's (DODIG) is responsible for conducting and overseeing military whistleblower reprisal investigations. This book examines the extent to which DOD met statutory notification and internal timeliness requirements for completing military whistleblower reprisal investigations; DODIG's whistleblower case management system supports oversight of reprisal investigations; and DOD has processes to ensure oversight of service IG-conducted reprisal investigations. It also describes best practices for conducting military reprisal and restriction intakes and investigations.

In: Military Whistleblower Reprisal … ISBN: 978-1-63483-938-9
Editor: Jesse L. Porter

Chapter 1

WHISTLEBLOWER PROTECTION DOD NEEDS TO ENHANCE OVERSIGHT OF MILITARY WHISTLEBLOWER REPRISAL INVESTIGATIONS*

United States Government Accountability Office

WHY GAO DID THIS STUDY

Whistleblowers play an important role in safeguarding the federal government against waste, fraud, and abuse. However, reporting wrongdoing outside the chain of command conflicts with military guidance, which emphasizes using the chain of command to resolve problems. Whistleblowers who make a report risk reprisal from their unit, such as being demoted or separated. DODIG is responsible for conducting and overseeing military whistleblower reprisal investigations. GAO was asked to examine DOD's oversight of military whistleblower reprisal investigations.

This report examines the extent to which (1) DOD met statutory notification and internal timeliness requirements for completing military whistleblower reprisal investigations, (2) DODIG's whistleblower case management system supports oversight of reprisal investigations, and (3) DOD

* This is an edited, reformatted and augmented version of a United States Government Accountability Office publication, No. GAO-15-477, dated May 2015.

has processes to ensure oversight of service IG-conducted reprisal investigations. GAO analyzed DODIG and service IG data for cases closed in fiscal years 2013 and 2014 and cases open as of September 30, 2014, and reviewed a generalizable random sample of 124 military reprisal cases closed in fiscal year 2013.

WHAT GAO RECOMMENDS

GAO recommends that DOD develop a tool to help ensure compliance with the statutory notification requirement, develop an implementation plan for expanding DODIG's case management system, and issue guidance governing the oversight process, among other things. DOD concurred, but raised issues with GAO's presentation of its findings. GAO disagrees and addresses these issues in this report.

WHAT GAO FOUND

The Department of Defense (DOD) did not meet statutory military whistleblower reprisal 180-day notification requirements in about half of reprisal investigations closed in fiscal year 2013, and DOD's average investigation time for closed cases in fiscal years 2013 and 2014 was 526 days, almost three times DOD's internal 180-day requirement. In 2012, GAO made recommendations to improve investigation timeliness, and DOD has taken some actions to address those recommendations. However, based on a random sample of 124 cases, GAO estimated that there was no evidence that DOD sent the required notification letters in about 47 percent of the cases that DOD took longer than 180 days to close in fiscal year 2013. For cases in which DOD sent the required letter, GAO estimated that the median notification time was about 353 days after the servicemember filed the complaint, and on average the letters significantly underestimated the expected investigation completion date. DOD does not have a tool, such as an automated alert, to help ensure compliance with the statutory notification requirement to provide letters by 180 days informing servicemembers about delays in investigations. Without a tool for DOD to ensure that servicemembers receive reliable, accurate, and timely information about their investigations, servicemembers may be discouraged from reporting wrongdoing.

DOD's Office of Inspector General's (DODIG) newly developed case management system, which it established to improve monitoring, is separate from the service IGs' systems, limiting DODIG's ability to provide oversight of all military reprisal investigations. GAO found that DODIG's system did not have a record of at least 22 percent of service-conducted reprisal investigations that were closed in fiscal years 2013 and 2014 and investigations open as of September 30, 2014. DODIG officials stated that they plan to expand DODIG's case management system to the service IGs by the end of fiscal year 2016 to improve DODIG's visibility over investigations. However, DODIG does not have an implementation plan for the expansion, and service IG officials stated that they have unique requirements that they would like to have incorporated into the system prior to expansion. Expanding the case management system to the service IGs without developing an implementation plan that, among other things, addresses the needs of both DODIG and the service IGs, puts DOD at risk of creating a system that will not strengthen its oversight of reprisal investigations.

DOD does not have formalized processes to help ensure effective oversight of military whistleblower reprisal investigations conducted by service IGs. DODIG established an oversight investigator team to review service IG investigations, but it has provided oversight investigators with limited guidance on how to review or document service IG investigations. Specifically, GAO estimated that for about 45 percent of service investigations closed in fiscal year 2013, the oversight worksheets were missing narrative to demonstrate that the oversight investigator had thoroughly documented all case deficiencies or inconsistencies. GAO also found that these files did not include documentation of DOD's analysis of the effect of noted deficiencies on the investigation's outcome because DOD has provided limited instruction on how to review service IG cases. Without additional guidance on oversight review procedures and documentation requirements to formalize the oversight process, it will be difficult for DOD to ensure that reprisal complaints are investigated and documented consistently.

ABBREVIATIONS

BCMR	Boards for the Correction of Military Records
CIGIE	Council of the Inspectors General on Integrity and Efficiency
DOD	Department of Defense
DODIG	Department of Defense Inspector General

GAGAS	Generally Accepted Government Auditing Standards
IG	Inspector General

* * *

May 7, 2015

Congressional Requesters

Whistleblowers play an important role in safeguarding the federal government against waste, fraud, and abuse, and their willingness to come forward can contribute to improvements in government operations. However, reporting wrongdoing outside the chain of command conflicts with military culture and service guidance, which emphasizes the importance of using the chain of command to resolve problems. Once military whistleblowers decide to make a report of wrongdoing they risk reprisal from their unit, such as being demoted, reassigned, or separated. According to the 2014 Federal Employee Viewpoint Survey, 18 percent of Department of Defense (DOD) employees surveyed did not feel they could disclose a suspected violation of any law, rule, or regulation without fear of reprisal.[1] Moreover, within the Department of Defense Office of Inspector General (DODIG), a quarter of employees surveyed in 2014 did not feel they could disclose a suspected violation of any law, rule, or regulation without fear of reprisal.[2]

In February 2012, we found that DODIG's oversight of the military whistleblower reprisal program faced challenges. For example, we found that DODIG was not consistently or accurately recording key dates to track the length of investigations, DOD was not meeting timeliness requirements for reporting on military whistleblower reprisal investigations, and DODIG did not report reprisal investigation timeliness data to Congress.[3] We recommended, and DOD concurred, that DOD needed to implement policies and procedures to ensure accurate and complete recording and consistent tracking of total case-processing time, track and analyze timeliness data, and regularly report investigation timeliness to Congress, among other things. DOD has taken some action to implement these recommendations, as discussed later in the report.[4]

You asked us to examine DOD's oversight of military whistleblower reprisal investigations. Specifically, this report examines the extent to which (1) DOD has met statutory notification and internal timeliness requirements for completing military whistleblower reprisal investigations; (2) DODIG's whistleblower case management system supports oversight of the military whistleblower reprisal program; and (3) DOD has processes to ensure oversight of military whistleblower reprisal investigations conducted by the service Offices of Inspectors General (IG).[5]

For our first objective, we obtained DODIG's data on all military whistleblower reprisal cases closed from October 1, 2012, through September 30, 2014, and all cases open as of October 1, 2014.[6] These data include all cases that were received from October 1, 2012, through September 30, 2014. We calculated the timeliness of cases using these data and compared the average timeliness to requirements outlined in statute and DOD directives. We assessed the reliability of the data by comparing electronic data to case-file documentation and interviewing DODIG officials responsible for the data, and we determined the data were sufficiently reliable for the purposes of this report. We also reviewed relevant documentation, such as standard operating procedures and investigative guidance from DODIG, and the service IGs for the Army, the Navy, the Air Force, and the Marine Corps. Finally, we interviewed officials from these offices about methods for tracking investigations and processes for sending required notifications to servicemembers that allege reprisal. We also spoke with officials from DODIG's Information Systems directorate to determine which variables to request from DODIG's case management system.

For the second objective, we collected and compared data from each of the service IGs to DODIG's data, to determine to what extent DODIG has visibility of all ongoing military whistleblower reprisal cases and cases closed from October 1, 2012, through September 30, 2014. Specifically, we matched selected variables for all cases from DODIG's data to the service IG data for those cases in order to identify duplicate cases and missing information. We selected the servicemember name, case identifiers, open date, and closed date—the variables present in both DODIG's and the service IGs' data—in consultation with DODIG and service officials. We assessed the reliability of the service data by reviewing related documentation and interviewing responsible service officials, and we determined the data were sufficiently reliable for the purposes of this report. In addition, we collected relevant documentation, such as case management system user manuals, and interviewed officials from the service IGs for the Army, the Navy, the Air Force, and the Marine Corps about guidance available for using their respective systems. Further, we reviewed documentation about the development of DODIG's case management system, including cost information for the next phase of development, and DOD memorandums regarding the case management system expansion. We also interviewed DODIG officials responsible for the development of the case management system and the proposed expansion of DODIG's case management system, which DODIG established to improve its monitoring of investigations. We compared this information to relevant program-management criteria.[7]

For our third objective, we selected a stratified random sample of 124 case files from the population of 498 case files retained by DODIG for military whistleblower reprisal cases that DODIG closed in fiscal year 2013, that is, from October 1, 2012, through September 30, 2013. We chose cases from this period for the file review because of DODIG's case management system transition in December 2012 and because the National Defense Authorization Act for Fiscal Year 2014, effective December 26, 2013, expanded the amount of time a servicemember has to report a reprisal allegation from 60 days to 1 year. We reviewed each selected case file to identify case characteristics, determine whether there was documentation that DOD had oversight mechanisms in place, and determine the extent to which the investigations aligned with quality standards for investigations established by the Council of the Inspectors General on Integrity and Efficiency (CIGIE).[8] To complete the case-file review, we developed a data-collection instrument to record case-file information regarding general case characteristics, timeliness, case-file completeness, and qualitative factors, such as investigation deficiencies recorded on DODIG's oversight worksheets. Two analysts independently reviewed each case file to help ensure the accuracy of the information in the data-collection instrument. These analysts discussed any areas of disagreement and resolved the disagreement by identifying and reviewing supporting documentation in the case files. We did not question DODIG's judgment in these cases. For example, we reviewed and assessed the files, but did not question DODIG's judgments, findings, or final determinations regarding whether to substantiate a reprisal allegation in any of the cases. We generalized the results of our sample to the population of 498 cases closed in fiscal year 2013, and all estimates of percentages presented in this report have a margin of error of plus or minus 10 percentage points or fewer, unless otherwise noted.

All estimates of medians and averages presented in this report have a relative error of plus or minus 20 percent of the estimate, unless otherwise noted.

We also interviewed all the investigators and supervisors on DODIG's military whistleblower reprisal oversight team, and randomly selected investigators at the service IGs and field-level investigators from the Army, the Navy, and the Air Force IGs to obtain information on procedures for reprisal investigations and oversight.[9] While the information from the investigators is not generalizable to all headquarters or field-level investigators, it provided us with additional perspectives into the service-specific processes for reprisal investigations. Further, we attended training sessions and reviewed training materials and requirements for investigators as well as processes for assessing investigator independence at DODIG and the service IGs. Additional details about our scope and methodology are discussed in appendix I.

We conducted this performance audit from April 2014 to May 2015 in accordance with generally accepted government auditing standards. Those standards require that we plan and perform the audit to obtain sufficient, appropriate evidence to provide a reasonable basis for our findings and conclusions based on our audit objectives. We believe that the evidence obtained provides a reasonable basis for our findings and conclusions based on our audit objectives.

BACKGROUND

DOD Policies on Military Whistleblower Reprisal Are Governed by Statute

In 1988, Congress enacted the Military Whistleblower Protection Act to provide protection to servicemembers who report wrongdoing within DOD.[10] According to DOD policy, a military whistleblower is a servicemember who makes, prepares to make, or is perceived as making or preparing to make a protected communication—that is, a report of a violation of law or regulation, gross waste of funds, or abuse of authority, among others, to an authorized individual or organization.[11]

An authorized individual includes, among others, a Member of Congress, an IG, and any person or organization in the servicemember's chain of command. Further, any lawful communication to a Member of Congress or IG is protected.[12] Reprisal occurs when a responsible management official takes, threatens to take, withholds, or threatens to withhold a personnel action because a servicemember made or was preparing to make a protected communication.

A personnel action is any action taken on a servicemember that affects or has the potential to affect a servicemember's current position or career, such as an adverse performance evaluation, letter of reprimand, or separation from service, among others.

Servicemembers and former servicemembers may submit reprisal complaints to DODIG or an IG within DOD. In 2013, Congress expanded the time for servicemembers to file a reprisal complaint from 60 days to 1 year following the date on which the servicemember becomes aware of the personnel action.[13] While the law affords military whistleblowers certain protections, those who allege they have suffered reprisal generally do not receive relief from the alleged reprisal until DOD has completed an investigation and substantiated the claims of reprisal.

DODIG and Service IGs Have Responsibility for Investigating Military Whistleblower Reprisal Complaints

DODIG can conduct an investigation into a military reprisal complaint or refer the investigation to the appropriate service IG; however, according to DOD policy, no determination is complete without final approval from DODIG. Whistleblower Reprisal Investigations is the directorate within DODIG's Administrative Investigations component that is responsible for conducting and overseeing investigations of reprisal and restriction complaints filed by servicemembers.

According to DOD policy, the Whistleblower Reprisal Investigations directorate is to approve service IG recommendations to dismiss cases, review and approve the results of investigations conducted by the service IGs, and initiate follow-up investigations to correct any inadequacies in service IG investigations.[14] The majority of DODIG's investigation workload for military reprisal cases is related to oversight reviews of investigations conducted by the service IGs. The directorate is also responsible for investigating reprisal complaints filed by DOD civilian employees, and employees of DOD contractors and subcontractors, among others. According to DODIG's semiannual reports to Congress, military whistleblower reprisal complaints account for approximately 60 percent of the reprisal complaints it receives. Figure 1 provides a summary of the investigation process, as described in DODIG guidance.

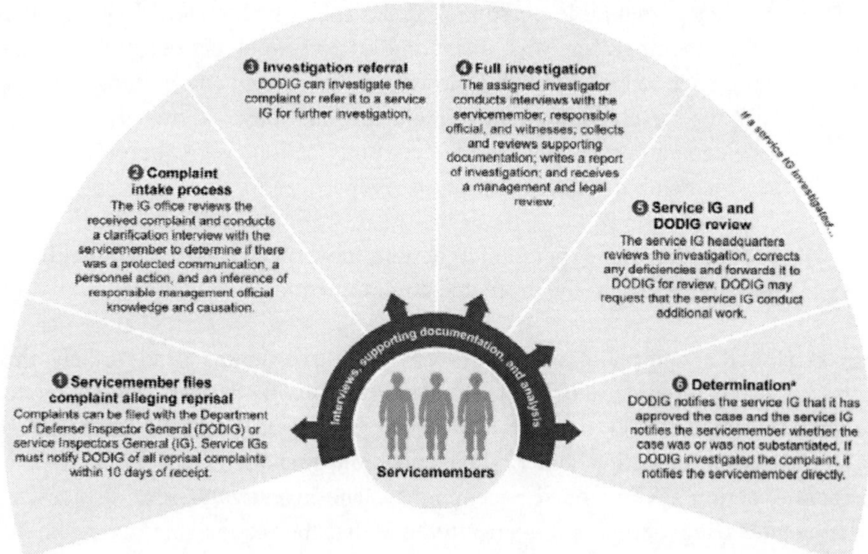

Source: GAO analysis of DODIG information. | GAO-15-477.

[a]If DODIG substantiates the reprisal complaint, the servicemember may separately apply to his or her military department's Board for the Correction of Military Records to receive relief from the unfavorable personnel action(s). The Boards for the Correction of Military Records are military department organizations with responsibility for reviewing and taking action on applications for the correction of military records at the request of a servicemember.

Figure 1. Military Whistleblower Reprisal Investigation Process.

DOD's Military Whistleblower Reprisal Investigative Process Focuses on Identifying Four Elements of Reprisal

According to DODIG's *Guide to Investigating Military Whistleblower Reprisal and Restriction Complaints*, DODIG and service IG investigators are to assess reprisal complaints by answering four questions to determine whether the elements of reprisal are present.[15] Specifically:

1) Did the servicemember make or prepare to make a protected communication, or was the servicemember perceived as having made or prepared to make a protected communication?

2) Was an unfavorable personnel action taken or threatened against the servicemember, or was a favorable personnel action withheld or threatened to be withheld, following the protected communication?
3) Did the responsible management official have knowledge of the servicemember's protected communication or perceive the servicemember as making or preparing to make a protected communication?
4) Would the same personnel action have been taken, withheld, or threatened absent the protected communication?

During the complaint intake process, the investigator is to review the complaint and timeline and conduct an interview with the servicemember to determine whether (1) the servicemember made or prepared to make a protected communication and (2) a responsible management official took a personnel action against the servicemember. The investigator is to also assess whether the allegation supports an inference that the responsible management official had knowledge of the protected communication and suggests a causal connection between the protected communication and the personnel action, such as whether the personnel action closely followed the protected communication. If the investigating officer determines there was no protected communication, no personnel action, or no inference of responsible management official knowledge or causation, the investigating officer can recommend that DODIG dismiss the case.

If a servicemember's complaint contains a personnel action and a protected communication, and an inference of knowledge and causation, the case is to proceed to a full investigation, according to DODIG guidance.[16] When determining whether the responsible management official would have taken the personnel action if the servicemember had not made a protected communication, the investigating officer is to determine the official's reasons for taking the action, the timing between the protected communication and the personnel action, the official's motive, and whether the servicemember was treated differently than other servicemembers who did not make protected communications. The investigating officer is to determine the case outcome based on a "preponderance of the evidence," defined by DODIG as the degree of relevant evidence that a reasonable person, considering the record as a whole, would accept as sufficient to find that a contested fact is more likely to be true than untrue.

According to DODIG guidance, if the investigating officer finds: (1) that the servicemember made a protected communication, and that the responsible management official (2) took a personnel action against the servicemember following the protected communication, (3) had knowledge of the protected communication, and (4) would not have taken the personnel action without the protected communication, the investigator writes a report that substantiates the reprisal complaint. After the investigator completes the report, it is subject to DODIG supervisory and managerial review and approval, as well as a legal sufficiency review. If the investigation is conducted by a service IG investigator, the service IG headquarters reviews and forwards the report to DODIG for oversight and final approval. In cases where DODIG substantiates a reprisal complaint, the servicemember may take an additional step to petition the appropriate Board for the Correction of Military Records for relief from the personnel action.[17]

DOD Did Not Always Meet Statutory Notification and Internal Timeliness Requirements for Completing Military Whistleblower Reprisal Investigations

DOD did not meet statutory notification requirements to inform servicemembers about delays in investigations for about half of military whistleblower reprisal investigations in fiscal year 2013. Further, in the notifications that DOD sent, reasons about the delays were general in nature and projected report completion dates were, on average, significantly underestimated. In addition, DOD rarely met internal timeliness requirements for completing military whistleblower reprisal investigations within 180 days for cases that it did not dismiss at intake. The average length of an investigation during fiscal years 2013 and 2014 was almost three times the DOD requirement.

DOD Did Not Meet Statutory Notification Requirements for about Half of Reprisal Investigations in Fiscal Year 2013

According to 10 U.S.C. § 1034 if, during the course of the investigation, the IG determines that it is not possible to submit the report of investigation to the Secretary of Defense and the service Secretary within 180 days after the receipt of the allegation, the IG shall provide to the Secretary of Defense, the service Secretary concerned, and the servicemember making the allegation a notice of that determination including the reasons why the report may not be submitted within that time and an estimate of the time when the report will be submitted. DODIG considers its office to be in accordance with the statute as long as it either completes the investigation within 180 days or submits a letter to the servicemember within 180 days, according to a senior DODIG official. In February 2012, we found that DODIG officials acknowledged that they and the service IGs had not been making the required notifications, but that they were taking steps to ensure that they met statutory notification requirements.[18] For example, in February 2012, DODIG issued policy guidance to the service IGs reemphasizing the statutory requirement to notify servicemembers if investigations are not completed within 180 days.[19] Further, according to oversight investigators we spoke with, they are to determine whether the service IG sent the 180-day notification letter as part of DODIG's oversight review of service IG-investigated cases and in fiscal year 2013, it was included as an item on DODIG's oversight worksheet for oversight investigators to look for during their oversight review. DODIG officials stated that they have taken additional action to ensure they meet statutory notification requirements since fiscal year 2013, which was the time frame covered by our case-file review. Specifically, in fall 2013, DODIG assigned an oversight investigator to periodically reconcile 180-day notification letters with the service IGs to ensure that the service IGs have sent the required letters and that DODIG has received a copy, according to DODIG officials. In addition, DODIG developed a mechanism in its case management system to indicate which cases are older than 180 days. However, DOD officials told us they have not developed a tool, such as an automated alert, to proactively ensure that they are in compliance with the statutory 180-day notification requirement.

On the basis of our file review of a stratified random sample of 124 cases closed by DODIG in fiscal year 2013, we found that DOD has made improvements related to these reporting requirements and that some case files that required letters contained evidence that DOD had sent the letters. However, we estimate that about 47 percent of the files for cases that DOD took longer than 180 days to close in fiscal year 2013 did not contain evidence that the investigating IG sent the required letters to servicemembers.[20] In addition, we found that in cases in which DODIG or the service IG sent the required letter, it typically did so after the case had reached the 180-day mark. Based on our file review, we estimate that for cases in which DODIG or the service IG sent a 180-day notification letter to the servicemember to explain the delays in the investigation, the median notification time was about 353 days after the servicemember filed the complaint.[21] In some service investigations, the investigating IG did not send the required letter to the servicemember until it forwarded the report of investigation to DODIG for review, more than 1 year after the servicemember filed the complaint.

Further, the letters that DOD sent provided general reasons for the delay, but, on average, significantly underestimated the date by which it would complete the investigation. For example, reasons for the investigation delay included case complexity, case volume, and delays that the service IG experienced in coordinating information, witnesses, and testimony. Based on the results of our file review, we estimate that the median time for case completion stated by DODIG and the service IGs in the letters, which they sent, on average, around 353 days into the investigation, was about an additional 78 days.[22] However, we estimate that for cases in which the investigating IG sent the required letter, the median time for case closure was actually 488 days, 57 days past the stated estimate for case completion.

Service IG officials stated that, for most cases over 180 days, they provide a standard estimate for case completion because it is difficult to estimate the amount of time required for case completion due to the unique characteristics of each case and the number of layers of review prior to case closure. According to federal standards for internal control, an agency must have relevant, reliable, and timely communications relating to internal and external events in order to determine whether the agency is achieving its compliance with various laws and regulations. 23 On the basis of our file review, we estimate that, on average, the notifications present in 53 percent of investigations closed in fiscal year 2013 in which they were required were untimely and contained unreliable estimates. Figure 2 shows the median notification timeframes and estimates for case completion for fiscal year 2013 cases over 180 days.

Although, as mentioned previously, DOD has taken steps to improve its notification process since 2012, without a tool—such as an automated mechanism to alert DOD that certain investigations are approaching the 180-day mark—to ensure that it is in compliance with the statutory 180- day notification requirement, servicemembers may not have reliable and accurate information about their reprisal investigations. Such information may affect the servicemembers' immediate work environment or personnel actions, which are typically halted during an active investigation, according to officials.

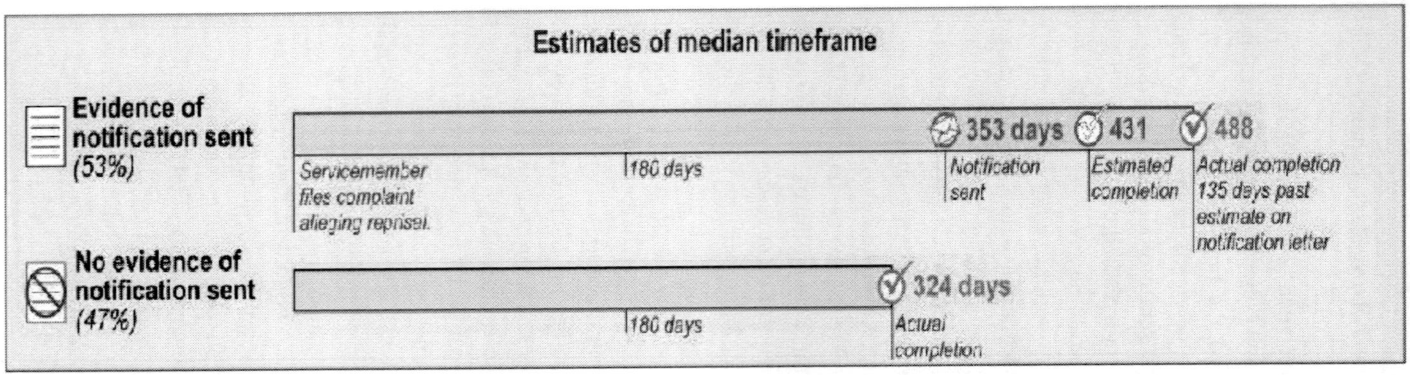

Source: GAO analysis of Department of Defense Inspector General (DODIG) military whistleblower case files closed in fiscal year 2013. | GAO-15-477.

Note: All percentage estimates in this figure have a margin of error of plus or minus 10 percentage points or fewer and all estimated medians have a relative margin of error of plus or minus 22 percent of the estimate or less.

Figure 2. Estimated Servicemember Median Notification Timelines for Military Whistleblower Cases Closed in Fiscal Year 2013 and over 180 Days.

Service IG officials stated that while servicemembers are protected as whistleblowers under the statute, they do not receive relief from reprisal until DODIG has completed and approved a substantiated investigation. Therefore, servicemembers would benefit from a status update from DOD within 180 days of receipt of an allegation with accurate information regarding their complaint. Further, as we reported in January 2015, status updates provide reassurance to whistleblowers during the investigative process, and without status updates, whistleblowers can become discouraged and develop a negative view of the process, according to officials. Specifically, a senior DODIG official stated that, at a minimum, a status update regarding progress toward case completion provides the servicemember with an element of assurance that the case is being actively worked on and has not slipped through the cracks.[24] Ultimately, the absence of a status update may discourage servicemembers from coming forward to report wrongdoing.

DOD's Military Whistleblower Reprisal Investigations Took Almost Three Times DOD's Internal Timeliness Requirement in Fiscal Years 2013 and 2014

DOD rarely met internal timeliness requirements for completing military whistleblower reprisal investigations in fiscal years 2013 and 2014. According to DOD Directive 7050.06, which implements the statute 10 U.S.C. § 1034 and establishes DOD policy, DODIG shall issue a whistleblower reprisal investigation report—containing a thorough review of the facts and circumstances, relevant documents acquired, and summaries or transcripts of interviews conducted—within 180 days of the receipt of the allegation of reprisal.

We found that the average investigation time for all cases that DOD (that is, both DODIG and the service IGs) investigated and closed in fiscal years 2013 and 2014 was 526 days.[25] The average length of DODIGinvestigated cases closed in fiscal years 2013 and 2014 was 443 days. The average length of service IG–investigated cases during this time was 530 days, which is almost three times DOD's internal timeliness requirement.[26] For cases DODIG dismissed after completing the complaint intake process, the average processing time was 48 days.[27] See table 1 for details regarding case-processing times for cases closed by DODIG and the service IGs in fiscal years 2013 and 2014.

Table 1. Processing Time for Military Whistleblower Reprisal Cases by Investigating Organization for Cases Closed in Fiscal Years 2013 and 2014

Investigating Inspector General (IG)	Minimum days	Maximum days	Mean days	Median days	Percentage of cases over 180 days
Department of Defense Inspector General (DODIG)	117	1000	443	386	92%
Army IG	21	2353	618	543	89
Air Force IG	73	1659	448	386	86
Naval IG	62	1171	452	420	81
Marine Corps IG	236	546	339	316	100
Other[a]	60	896	423	422	91
All service IG investigations	21	2353	530	464	87%
All DOD investigations	21	2353	526	455	87%

Source: GAO analysis of DODIG data. | GAO-15-477.

[a]Other includes investigations conducted by the IGs of the Joint Staff, Coast Guard, defense agencies, and combatant commands.

In our total timeliness calculations for all DOD investigations, we did not include complaints that DODIG or the service IGs dismissed at intake because the IG determined that the complaint did not have sufficient evidence to warrant an investigation. While the statute requires the service IG receiving the reprisal allegation to promptly notify DODIG of the allegation, services do not consistently provide DODIG notification when they receive complaints that do not contain a protected communication or personnel action, according to service IG officials and guidance. Specifically, the Air Force IG's guidance states that DODIG must be notified when a complaint contains an allegation of reprisal. However, the guidance states that a complaint does not contain a reprisal allegation unless the first two elements of reprisal—a protected communication and a personnel action—are present. DODIG officials stated that any service determination that a complaint does not meet its first two elements of reprisal must be submitted to DODIG for oversight. However, officials from the two service IGs, which accounted for approximately 80 percent of the service IG reprisal investigative workload in fiscal years 2013 and 2014 told us that they do not track or report to DODIG complaints that they dismiss at intake because they lacked a protected communication or personnel action. Since DODIG does not have data on cases that the services dismiss at intake, because the services do not notify them of these cases, we did not have data on all cases that were dismissed at intake. Therefore we reported the timeliness of cases that DODIG dismissed at intake separately, and did not include them in our overall timeliness calculations.

In fiscal years 2013 and 2014, DODIG investigated and closed a total of 39 cases and dismissed another 375 complaints after completing the intake process. The service IGs closed a total of 674 cases during this period. See table 2 for the number of cases closed by each investigating organization in fiscal years 2013 and 2014.

Table 2. Number of Military Whistleblower Reprisal Cases Closed by Investigating Organization in Fiscal Years 2013 and 2014

Investigating Inspector General (IG)	Cases closed in fiscal year 2013	Cases closed in fiscal year 2014	Total cases closed in fiscal years 2013 and 2014
Department of Defense Inspector General (DODIG)	16	23	39
Army IG	128	206	334
Air Force IG	105	97	202
Naval IG	52	62	114
Marine Corps IG	3	10	13
Other[a]	10	1	11
Total	314	399	713

Source: GAO analysis of DODIG data. | GAO-15-477

Note: DODIG dismissed an additional 166 cases in fiscal year 2013 and 209 cases in fiscal year 2014 at intake.

[a]Other includes investigations conducted by the IGs of the Joint Staff, Coast Guard, defense agencies, and combatant commands.

DOD received a total of 640 reprisal complaints in fiscal year 2013 and 584 reprisal complaints in fiscal year 2014. As of September 30, 2014, DODIG and the service IGs had a total of 822 open military whistleblower reprisal cases. While the majority of these open cases were filed from fiscal years 2012 through 2014, some of these cases had been open since fiscal year 2008. We found that almost 20 percent of DOD's open military reprisal cases were filed in fiscal year 2012 and had been open for at least 2 years. Further, approximately 33 percent of the open military reprisal cases were filed in 2013 and had been open for at least 1 year. Table 3 provides additional information on DOD's open military reprisal cases and when the servicemembers filed their reprisal complaints. Appendix II provides information about substantiation rates and the general characteristics of military whistleblower reprisal cases.

Table 3. Open Military Whistleblower Reprisal Cases by Fiscal Year in Which Complaints Were Filed, as of September 30, 2014

Fiscal year filed	Cases open	Percentage of open cases
2008	3	0.4%
2009	4	0.5
2010	5	0.6
2011	24	2.9
2012	163	19.8
2013	267	32.5
2014	356	43.3
Total	**822**	**100%**

Source: GAO analysis of Department of Defense Inspector General (DODIG) data. | GAO-15-477.

DOD officials described several factors affecting the timeliness of military reprisal investigations and stated that they are taking steps to improve investigation timeliness. For example, in addition to investigations, DODIG's workload includes completing the intake process for complaints filed with DODIG. Intake requires staff to review complaints and determine whether there is sufficient evidence for those complaints to warrant an investigation. As we stated previously, DODIG dismissed 375 complaints after completing the intake process in fiscal years 2013 and 2014. Further, service IG officials indicated that the decentralized investigation structure is a factor that affects the timeliness of their investigations. For example, service IGs assign investigations to field-level investigators, which, according to officials, results in a multilayer review process as the investigation is reviewed by each organizational level of the service with each layer of review adding to case-processing times. Additionally, all six field-level service investigators we interviewed stated that, in their opinion,180 days was not a reasonable amount of time to complete all investigations unless an investigator has no competing responsibilities and is able to focus solely on one reprisal investigation at a time. Service IG investigators further stated that in addition to competing responsibilities, the complexity of cases, the volume of cases, and low staffing numbers all affect the timeliness of investigations. We found in February 2012 that DODIG also identified staffing shortages as a factor affecting the timely processing of cases and that staffing levels had not kept up with an increased reprisal caseload.[28]

DODIG officials stated that they have increased their personnel levels to accommodate the increased caseload. Specifically, DODIG's Whistleblower Reprisal Investigations directorate increased from 30 staff in January 2012 to 53 staff in March 2015.

Further, DODIG officials stated that DOD leadership has made improving the timeliness of administrative investigations—which include both investigations of whistleblower reprisal and of other allegations made against senior officials—a priority. Specifically, in an effort to improve the timeliness of senior official investigations, including senior official whistleblower reprisal cases, DODIG convened a timeliness task force in coordination with the service IGs, which issued a report with recommendations in November 2014. Specifically, the task force recommended that DODIG expand its case management system to track and manage the timeliness of senior official investigations. DODIG officials stated that they believe the expansion of the case management system will improve timeliness for all reprisal investigations. Following the issuance of the task force's report, in January 2015, the Deputy Secretary of Defense issued a memorandum endorsing the findings of the report, specifically stating that the service IGs should not impose any staffing reductions on the investigation offices because they must be adequately resourced when faced with multiple high-priority investigations.[29]

In February 2012, we made three recommendations to DODIG to improve timeliness: (1) implement policies and procedures to ensure accurate and complete recording and consistent tracking of total case-processing time, (2) track and analyze timeliness data to identify reforms that could aid in processing cases within 180 days, and (3) regularly report to Congress on the timeliness of military whistleblower reprisal investigations.[30] DOD concurred with these recommendations. Although DODIG has taken some actions to address the recommendations, DODIG has not fully implemented them. Specifically, DODIG developed a case management system in December 2012 to use to collect key dates to track the timeliness of DODIG investigative phases. DODIG's case management system contains a metric to calculate total case time of service IG investigations from receipt of complaint to servicemember notification of the final outcome. DODIG officials stated that they use this metric to track timeliness for service IG reprisal investigations. However, according to officials, this calculation is inaccurate for cases opened prior to the case management system being implemented in December 2012, which accounts for approximately 24 percent of open investigations. Specifically, based on the results of our file review, we estimate that the timeliness metric in DODIG's case management system underestimates total case time for each case closed in fiscal year 2013 by at least 26 days on average, which limits DODIG's ability to monitor the timeliness of all service IG investigations.[31] DODIG officials stated that they are able to identify the cases that are affected by the inaccurate timeliness metric and that they have implemented processes to manually calculate the case age for these cases.

Further, as we discuss later in this report, DOD has not implemented procedures to ensure accurate and complete recording of total case-processing time. DODIG collects timeliness information but cannot analyze the data to identify potential reforms because the case management system is under development and has limited reporting capabilities. In addition, the service IGs have separate case management systems; therefore the timeliness of all service investigative phases is not maintained in DODIG's case management system, which does not allow DODIG to consistently track all case processing times. Finally, DODIG responds to ad hoc congressional requests related to investigation timeliness, but does not include overall timeliness information in its semiannual reports to Congress, as we recommended in February 2012. We continue to believe these recommendations are valid and should be implemented.

DODIG's New Case Management System Does Not Support Complete Oversight of Service Military Reprisal Investigations

DODIG implemented a new whistleblower reprisal investigation case management system to improve its monitoring of investigations; however, as of March 2015, the system is under development and has limited reporting capabilities. In addition, DODIG has provided its staff with limited user guidance on how to use and record information in the case management system. Further, DOD's use of multiple case management systems hinders its visibility over total workload and investigative activity at the service IG level, such as the number and status of military whistleblower reprisal investigations in process at the service IGs. DOD's planned expansion of its reprisal case management system to the service IGs may not result in improved visibility over its workload without further planning and guidance.

DODIG's New Case Management System to Improve Monitoring of Reprisal Investigations Is under Development

In February 2012, we found that DOD's efforts to improve case processing-times had been hindered by unreliable and incomplete data, and, as previously discussed, we recommended that DOD implement policies and procedures to ensure accurate and complete recording of case-processing time. DOD concurred with this recommendation.[32] In December 2012, DODIG took steps to improve its military whistleblower reprisal investigation data by implementing a new case management system to monitor its administrative investigations, including senior official and whistleblower reprisal investigations. We found the data from this case management system reliable for our purposes of reporting the average lengths of investigations for this report—an improvement since February 2012, when we reported that similar data from DODIG's previous system were not reliable for our reporting purposes. According to DODIG, the case management system is intended to streamline processing, investigations, and service IG oversight reviews by serving as an automated, real-time complaint tracking and investigative management tool that electronically stores all case-file documentation. However, as of March 2015, the case management system was under development and according to officials has limited reporting capabilities.

According to a DODIG official, DOD selected an incremental process to develop the case management system in order to incorporate user feedback into each phase of development, and, in accordance with this type of development, in December 2012 DODIG staff began using the case management system prior to the completion of the system. DODIG officials stated that they had planned to finish the development of the case management system by February 2014; however, according to these officials, DODIG delayed funding for the final development phase until fiscal year 2015, delaying the completion of the case management system. As a result of the delayed funding, DODIG has not been able to incorporate all user feedback to ensure that the case management system is fully functioning at the desired level, according to DODIG officials. For example, according to DODIG officials, the case management system's reporting capabilities are limited. The case management system contains the fields necessary to track the length of various investigative phases for DODIG investigations as we recommended in February 2012, such as the dates for the legal and internal review processes, but according to a DODIG official, it cannot track this information for service IG investigations. In addition, the case management system contains dashboards for users to manage cases by the whistleblower statutes for which DODIG is responsible. For example, users can view the dashboards to determine the number of investigations or oversight cases assigned to a particular investigator and the number of DODIG investigations over 180 days, among other things.

DODIG can also determine the length of time it took to complete these phases when users drill down to individual cases and review key dates for these phases in the investigation and oversight events tabs. However, according to DODIG officials, DODIG is not able to extract and aggregate these data from its case management system for analysis and reporting purposes, which would allow it to identify possible areas for implementing case-processing reforms, as we recommended in February 2012. DODIG officials stated that even though they have not completed the final development phase of the case management system, using the system has improved their ability to provide oversight of the service IG investigations, allowing them to track the corrective actions that services have taken in substantiated reprisal cases. Officials stated they can also calculate overall case age, the number of days to complete the intake phase, the number of days to complete the investigation phase, and the number of days in oversight, in response to findings in our previous report. However, DODIG can calculate these milestones only for cases that it investigates, which is a small portion of the military reprisal investigations on which this report focuses. In addition, as we previously stated, we found the case management system's field to calculate case age was inaccurate because it underestimates total case time for cases opened in the prior system and closed in fiscal year 2013 by at least 26 days on average.

Further, according to DODIG officials, DODIG spent approximately $2.22 million on the development of the case management system as of February 2015, and plans to spend approximately $1.4 million to further develop the case management system prior to the end of fiscal year 2015. DODIG officials stated that they plan to complete the final phase of case management system development, which includes improvements to reporting capabilities, by the end of fiscal year 2015. Other needed improvements include restrictions on which cases users can access and edit, as well as additional fields to better track specific types of case outcomes, such as cases withdrawn by servicemembers, according to DODIG officials. However, DODIG officials stated that they are unsure of the extent to which they will be able to make improvements to the case management system during the next phase of development given their current funding levels. As a result, DODIG officials stated that they have initiated a process to prioritize the improvements based on necessary and desired changes.

DODIG Provides Limited Guidance to Case Management System Users

DODIG has provided limited guidance to case management system users on how to populate case information into the new whistleblower reprisal case management system. DODIG investigators have been using the case management system to manage reprisal investigations since December 2012. As previously discussed, according to officials, DODIG planned to finish the final development phase for its case management system in February 2014, but changed that benchmark to September 2015.

According to an official, when the case management system was implemented, DODIG internally developed and provided its staff with a user manual. According to oversight investigators, guidance on the case management system is limited and does not include detailed operating instructions, such as the type of information to enter into the case notes fields. Further, one oversight investigator stated that the guidance DODIG provided before the system was implemented was minimal and included features of the system that were not yet operable. DODIG officials provided documentation of two types of guidance, a draft user manual created by Whistleblower Reprisal directorate staff with screen captures of the system, and desk aids for various staff positions that provide descriptions of the data fields the investigators are to complete. DODIG officials noted that they have issued several versions of the desk aids since they implemented the case management system. During our case file review, we found that DODIG investigators had incorrectly coded some cases in the case management system as fully investigated when the service IG had dismissed the case prior to a full investigation.

Based on the results of our file review, we estimate that, in fiscal year 2013, about 43 percent of cases that DODIG investigators coded as fully investigated were incorrectly coded in this way. Due to these miscoded cases, we are unable to report on the number of military whistleblower reprisal complaints that DOD fully investigated in fiscal years 2013 and 2014. In its semiannual reports to Congress, DODIG reports on the number of military whistleblower reprisal investigations fully investigated by DODIG and the service IGs. DODIG officials stated that they use their case management system to compile information for these semiannual reports. Based on our estimate of the number of cases affected by the miscoding in fiscal year 2013, DODIG may have mischaracterized its investigative work in its fiscal year 2013 semiannual reports to Congress. DODIG officials stated that they were aware that DODIG staff had improperly coded some reprisal cases as fully investigated when they were dismissed prior to a full investigation, but that they were not aware of the extent of the miscoding. Further, DODIG officials stated that they are taking steps to ensure that future cases are coded properly. For example, DODIG officials said that once they realized that DODIG staff were coding cases incorrectly, they provided desk aids to users in March 2014 that describe how to code cases that were fully investigated and those that were dismissed prior to a full investigation. However, during our case-file review we found that DODIG staff were still coding cases incorrectly as of April 2014. Further, in September 2013, DODIG assigned an Investigations Analyst to monitor its whistleblower reprisal investigations data. According to DODIG officials, the Investigations Analyst uses a dashboard in the case management system which helps identify missing data or entry errors, and then manually corrects them.

As previously discussed, DODIG's case management system is to serve as a real-time complaint tracking and investigative management tool for investigators within its Administrative Investigations component. Further, DODIG's fiscal year 2014 performance plan for oversight investigators notes that investigators should ensure the case management system reflects current, real-time information on case activity. However, based on our file review of a sample of 124 cases closed in fiscal year 2013, we found that DODIG investigators were not using the case management system for real-time case management as intended by DODIG officials. Specifically, we estimate that DODIG personnel uploaded key case documents to the case management system after DODIG had closed the case in 77 percent of cases closed in fiscal year 2013. For example, DODIG staff uploaded, among other things, reports of investigation, oversight worksheets, 180-day letters, and copies of the servicemembers' complaints after the case had already closed, indicating that the case management system was not being used for real-time case management at that time.

Further, we estimate that, for 83 percent of cases closed in fiscal year 2013, DODIG staff made changes to the case variables in the case management system in 2014, at least 3 months after case closure. For cases where DODIG made changes to the data, we estimate that about 68 percent had significant changes, such as changes to the date the servicemember filed the complaint and the organization that conducted the investigation, as well as the result code, which indicates whether the case was fully investigated. In explaining why the changes were made, DODIG officials stated that leadership from DODIG's Whistleblower Reprisal Investigations directorate instructed oversight investigators and other DODIG staff to verify and correct the data as necessary for all cases closed in fiscal years 2013 and 2014 by comparing case management system data to case file documentation. DODIG officials stated that this was necessary to ensure the reliability of DODIG's investigative data because the case management system was new to investigators and they had not been consistently recording information. Further, officials stated that prior to the implementation of the case management system, investigators reviewed hard-copy case files of service IG investigations and they did not immediately transition to reviewing case files electronically when the case management system was implemented in December 2012. The guidance DODIG has issued for the new case management system does not include instructions that the staff are to use the system for real-time case management and investigation review or which types of events to record, both of which could have helped guide the transition from hard-copy to electronic case file review.

DODIG officials stated that they plan to further develop their draft manual for the case management system expansion to the service IGs which they anticipate will be complete by the end of fiscal year 2016, as discussed later in the report. Officials further stated they will continue to update internal desk aides, which contain only descriptions of the case management system's fields, as needed, but do not plan to issue additional internal guidance for DODIG staff on the case management system because they believe that the current guidance is sufficient. However, DODIG's draft user manual does not instruct users on how to access the system, troubleshoot errors they may encounter, or monitor their caseloads using the case management systems dashboards. Further, DODIG's Administrative Investigations manual, which provides guidance to the Whistleblower Reprisal Investigations directorate staff, is outdated because it refers only to DODIG's prior case management system, which was replaced in December 2012.

According to CIGIE quality standards for investigations, accurate processing of information is essential to the mission of an investigative organization. It should begin with the orderly, systematic, accurate, and secure maintenance of a management information system. Written guidance should define the data elements to be recorded in the system. Further, management should have certain information available to perform its responsibilities, measure its accomplishments, and respond to requests by appropriate external customers.[33] DODIG officials stated that they plan to develop a user manual when they expand the case management system to service IGs, as discussed later in the report. Without updating and finalizing the internal user guidance from 2012 as necessary until the case management system is complete, including providing instructions on how to use the system as a real-time tracking system in the meantime, DODIG will continue to face challenges in its ability to report on the military whistleblower reprisal program. For example, unless investigators update and upload case information during the course of an investigation, DODIG will be unable to report on the real-time status of investigations and therefore may not be able to respond to congressional requests for case information without significant efforts. Further, DOD uses the case management system to compile information for reporting to Congress on its military reprisal investigation workload and thus may have inaccurately represented its workload—the number of cases fully investigated—to Congress in its semiannual reports. Without updating and finalizing internal guidance on how to correctly enter case information into the case management system, DODIG cannot ensure the reliability of its data without manually reviewing and correcting each case.

DOD Uses Multiple Decentralized Case Management Systems, Which Hinders Visibility, and Does Not Have an Implementation Plan for Expanding the DODIG Whistleblower Case Management System to the Service IGs

Each service IG conducts and monitors the status of military whistleblower reprisal investigations in a different case management system. Although DODIG has access to one of the service's case management systems, according to officials DODIG does not have complete visibility over service investigations from complaint receipt to investigation determination. As a result, DODIG may not know that some servicemembers have filed reprisal complaints until the service IGs forward the completed reports of investigation to DODIG for review. Further, DODIG does not have knowledge of the real-time status of service-conducted investigations and is unable to anticipate when service IGs will send completed reports of investigation for review, according to officials. DODIG is required to review all service IG determinations in military reprisal investigations in addition to its responsibility for conducting investigations of some military reprisal complaints. Without a common system to share data, DODIG's oversight of the timeliness of service investigations and visibility of its own future workload is limited.

Our analysis indicates that DODIG's case management system did not have record of at least 22 percent of service investigations both open as of September 30, 2014, and closed in fiscal years 2013 and 2014. According to DOD officials, DOD's decentralized structure for military reprisal investigations, paired with the fact that servicemembers can submit complaints to DOD or their respective service IG, or their chain of command, contributes to the possibility of duplicate complaints or that one IG fails to notify another of an ongoing reprisal investigation. According to DOD Directive 7050.06, when the service IGs receive reprisal complaints from servicemembers, those offices are required to notify DODIG within 10 days; however, based on our file review, we estimate that there was no evidence of this required notification in 30 percent of cases closed in fiscal year 2013 where the servicemember filed the complaint with the service IG.[34] In response, DODIG officials noted that one of their oversight investigators was assigned to reconcile DODIG's open military reprisal investigations with the service's open reprisal investigations in fall 2013. According to service IG officials, this reconciliation is conducted at various points throughout the year by manually comparing lists of investigations from each IG's respective case management system.

Through our analysis we identified challenges reconciling DODIG and services IG cases because the investigating organizations do not share a common case identifier. In addition, in fiscal years 2013 and 2014 each investigating organization did not consistently track the other organization's unique case identifier. DODIG officials stated that they have since taken steps to ensure that DODIG tracks the service IGs' case identifiers in its case management system. For example, the oversight investigator that DODIG assigned to reconcile cases updates service case identifiers in DODIG's case management system as part of the reconciliation process. Further, service IG officials stated that there have been instances where DODIG did not notify them that it was investigating a reprisal complaint from one of their servicemembers and they did not find out about the investigation until after DODIG had conducted the investigation. Standards for internal control in the federal government state that, for an entity to run and control its operations, it must have relevant, reliable, and timely communications relating to internal and external events.[35]

DOD is taking steps to improve its visibility over service investigations. In November 2014, a DODIG task force that focused on improving the timeliness of DOD's senior official investigations recommended that DOD expand the case management system to the service IGs as a way to improve investigation timeliness. According to DODIG officials, expanding the case management system is also an effort to improve DODIG's visibility of administrative investigations conducted by the service IGs. In January 2015, the Deputy Secretary of Defense endorsed the recommendation to expand the case management system to the service IGs, stating that an enterprise data system is essential to achieving a more seamless and efficient processing of complaints and investigations across the department. [36] With this endorsement, DODIG officials stated that they plan to expand the case management system to the service IGs by the end of fiscal year 2016.

However, DODIG does not have an implementation plan for the expansion and has not yet taken steps to develop one. According to DODIG officials, they are in the process of developing a strategy to expand the case management system and are in the early stages of the planning process. DODIG officials stated they have set an aggressive time frame for the expansion because leadership has made investigation timeliness a priority and they believe a common case management system is part of the solution. Officials stated that they have completed the process to classify the case management system as a defense business system in April 2014 and that DODIG has been using the system to process all whistleblower reprisal investigations since December 2012.[37] Further, officials stated that they developed a working group comprising representatives of each of the service IGs to facilitate planning for the expansion. The working group held its first meeting in February 2015, and plans to meet bimonthly until the expansion is complete. A DODIG official tasked with leading the expansion of the case management system stated that he intends to refer to best practices for project management to help facilitate the planning process for this expansion project.

The Project Management Institute's Guide to Project Management Body of Knowledge (PMBOK® Guide) provides guidelines for managing individual projects, including developing a project management plan. [38] A project management plan defines the basis of all project work, including how the project is executed, monitored and controlled, and closed. According to the PMBOK® Guide, project management plans should include a scope—to describe major deliverables, assumptions, and project constraints—project requirements, schedules, costs, stakeholder roles and responsibilities, and stakeholder communication techniques, among other things. Further, project management plans are to be updated when issues are found during the course of the project, which may modify project policies or procedures, and when actions are needed to forestall negative effects on the project.[39] Project management plans also include methods to define and document stakeholder needs. According to the Project Management Institute, detailed requirements documentation is essential for stakeholders to understand what needs to be (1) done to deliver the project and (2) produced as the result of the project.

DODIG officials stated that, in coordination with the service IGs, they will review and incorporate some needs of each service IG prior to expanding the case management system, but they do not plan to fully customize the case management system for each service IG, such as developing a different interface for each service. Service IG officials expressed concerns that they have requirements, such as specific data fields and report capabilities to meet leadership needs to be incorporated into the case management system prior to expansion. For example, service IG officials stated that it is important that case management system user roles are defined in a way that reflects how their organizations operate and that case access is restricted according to the organizational level of the user. Some service IG officials stated that they are concerned that DODIG will expand the case management system without incorporating all of their needs and that they will not be able to meet their respective service leaderships' reporting requirements as a result. These officials stated that if DODIG's case management system does not meet their needs they may need to continue to use their current case management systems, which would be duplicative.

Given DOD's stated plans to expand the case management system to the service IGs by the end of fiscal year 2016, doing so without developing an implementation plan that addresses the needs of DODIG and the service IGs, and defines project goals, schedules, costs, stakeholder roles and responsibilities, and stakeholder communication techniques, puts DODIG at risk of creating a system that will not improve its visibility over total workload or investigation timeliness. Further, without such a plan, DODIG may not be well-positioned to monitor the expansion and measure project success. In addition, without developing a plan in coordination with the service IGs that defines the roles and responsibilities of all stakeholders, and sets expectations for communication, DODIG may not be able to balance all stakeholder needs and interests. Further, as previously discussed, DODIG has not completed the development of the case management system and it does not meet DODIG user needs. Finally, in the absence of an implementation plan that adequately addresses the requirements of the service IGs, the service IGs may not know whether or when their needs will be met and as a result they may unnecessarily continue to use their own systems, which could be duplicative.

DOD Has Not Formalized Its Oversight Processes to Review Service IG Reprisal Investigations and to Help Ensure Investigation Quality and Independence

In 2011, DOD designated a team in DODIG's Directorate for Whistleblower Reprisal Investigations to review service-conducted investigations on a full-time basis; however, DODIG has not formalized the process for the review of military whistleblower reprisal investigations. For example, it is unclear to what extent DODIG has incorporated the relevant investigative standards into its process. Several factors affect the quality of DOD's oversight of service-conducted military whistleblower reprisal investigations, including the absence of standardized guidance and DODIG feedback to the service investigators. Finally, DOD does not have a tool for investigators to certify their independence to ensure its military whistleblower reprisal investigations are objective in fact and appearance.

DODIG Established an Oversight Team to Review Service-Investigated Reprisal Complaints, but the Oversight Process Is Not Formalized

In September 2011, DODIG took steps to improve its oversight of service IG investigations by establishing an investigator team that is solely dedicated to the oversight review of service IG-conducted military reprisal investigations, according to officials, but it has not formalized its process by providing detailed guidance to its oversight team. DODIG is responsible for reviewing and approving service determinations regarding whistleblower reprisal complaints, including both (1) service determinations that an investigation into a reprisal complaint is not warranted, and (2) the results of completed service reprisal investigations.[40] To improve oversight, DODIG officials said that they staffed the team with investigators who had experience at either DOD or service IGs. The oversight investigators are to document their review using an oversight worksheet, which captures information about how the service investigation was conducted as well as the investigation's findings and conclusions. DODIG has used various versions of this oversight worksheet since it established the oversight team. Our case-file review included case files closed in fiscal year 2013, and during this period DODIG's oversight worksheet was designed to capture information about (1) the servicemember's allegations of reprisal, (2) the personnel action or actions taken against the servicemember, (3) service investigation thoroughness, (4) documentation, (5) timeliness, (6) objectivity, and (7) whether there were any deficiencies or inconsistencies in the service investigation report, among other things.

DODIG and Service IG Adherence to CIGIE Standards

DODIG adheres to CIGIE standards, but the extent to which it incorporates these standards is unclear, and service IGs are not members of CIGIE. CIGIE's Quality Standards for Investigations provide a framework to help ensure high-quality investigations are conducted by member IG offices.[41] CIGIE's general standards apply to investigative organizations and include investigator qualifications, independence, and due professional care. CIGIE's qualitative standards relate to how the investigation is planned, executed, and reported, as well as how the investigative information is managed. As a CIGIE member, DODIG is expected to incorporate CIGIE's quality standards into its operations manuals or handbooks. Table 4 highlights some of the CIGIE standards that DODIG has incorporated into its oversight worksheet that investigators use to review service IG investigations.

Table 4. Summary of Council of the Inspectors General on Integrity and Efficiency (CIGIE) Quality Standards Identified by the Department of Defense Office of Inspector General (DODIG) in Reviews of Service Investigations

Quality standard	Definition	Questions DODIG is to answer when reviewing service investigations
Due Professional Care	• Thoroughness: Investigations must be conducted in a diligent and complete manner • Objectivity: Evidence is gathered and reported in an unbiased and independent manner	• Were all appropriate individuals interviewed? • Did the investigator ask appropriate open-ended questions during interviews? • Did the evidence support the investigationfindings?

Table 4. (Continued)

Quality standard	Definition	Questions DODIG is to answer when reviewing service investigations
	• Accurate and complete documentation: Report findings are supported by adequate documentation	
Independence	• Decisions used in obtaining evidence, conducting interviews, and making recommendations will be impartial and will be viewed as impartial by knowledgeable third parties	• Did the investigator demonstrate IG impartiality during interviews? • Was the investigator from outside the immediate chain of command?
Executing Investigations	• Evidence should be collected to ensure that all obviously relevant material is obtained •Investigations must comply with legal requirements	• Did the investigator gather all relevant evidence? • Did the report receive legal sufficiency review?
Reporting	• High-quality reports are logically organized, accurate, complete, impartial, and clear • In some cases investigators should note specific allegations that were not investigated	• Did the investigator accurately characterize the evidence? • Were emergent allegations addressed in this report?

Source: GAO analysis of DODIG and CIGIE data. | GAO-15-477

We found that DODIG's attestation to CIGIE standards, which is part of its oversight review, was inconsistent. For example, DODIG has changed the language on versions of its oversight worksheet between 2012 and 2014, and DODIG oversight investigators did not always attest to whether the investigations in our fiscal year 2013 sample were conducted in accordance with CIGIE standards. As a member of CIGIE, DODIG must develop and document its quality-control policies and procedures in accordance with its agency requirements, then communicate those policies and procedures to its personnel, according to CIGIE standards.[42] The oversight worksheet that DODIG was using as of March 2015 did not contain a block for CIGIE attestation, to indicate whether the investigation was conducted in accordance with CIGIE standards, but the worksheet asks whether the investigator gathered all relevant evidence and whether the investigator demonstrated IG impartiality during interviews. In contrast, the oversight worksheet that

DODIG oversight investigators used during the fiscal year 2013 time frame of our sample contained template language for the oversight investigator to indicate whether the service conducted the investigation in accordance with CIGIE standards, but the worksheets in our sample did not consistently attest to whether the approved investigation adhered to CIGIE standards, and the basis for the determination was unclear. Specifically, of the 89 service IG investigations in our sample, DODIG oversight investigators attested that 55 percent of them were conducted in accordance with CIGIE standards as reflected on the oversight worksheet.

Further, the service IGs are not members of CIGIE, and the service IG investigators are not subject or consistently trained to CIGIE standards. In 2012 DODIG hired a training officer and in 2013 developed a basic whistleblower reprisal investigations course for DODIG and service IG investigators. DODIG officials stated that they incorporated some CIGIE standards into this and other trainings as well as in their semiannual symposiums, but service IG officials stated that these DODIG-offered trainings do not reach all field-level investigators. A senior DODIG official stated that even though the service IGs are not subject to CIGIE standards, DODIG would not approve a service IG investigation that did not appear to adhere to CIGIE standards. Also, while DODIG's Administrative Investigations manual directs DODIG investigators to follow CIGIE standards, none of the DODIG-conducted military reprisal investigations in our sample included an attestation similar to the statement on the oversight worksheet for service IG cases stating they adhered to CIGIE standards.[43] DODIG officials stated that the attestation is not necessary for its own reprisal investigations because, as a CIGIE member, all of its investigations adhere to CIGIE standards.

DODIG Oversight Guidance and Instruction

DODIG provided the oversight team with limited instructions on how to review service IG cases. We interviewed each member of DODIG's oversight team to discuss their procedures for investigation review and found that they have different approaches for how they review investigations prior to completing the oversight worksheet. For example, some read the allegation of reprisal first, while others begin their oversight review by reading the service investigator's report of investigation. According to the oversight investigators we spoke to, once they review the investigation documentation and complete the oversight worksheet, they are to forward the package to their supervisors for discussion and review. For some cases, before final approval, oversight investigators discuss the oversight review during regular meetings with other oversight investigators, and with Whistleblower Reprisal Investigation management, according to officials. Finally, officials stated that management reviews some case files before DODIG issues the approval memo back to the service IG. DODIG officials stated that they have informal weekly meetings with the oversight team to discuss cases and oversight processes; however, some of the oversight investigators we spoke with noted that they had not received any detailed guidance that was specifically focused on how to conduct oversight of service IG military reprisal cases.

For the 89 oversight files in our sample, DODIG rarely disagreed with the service IG's final determination of whether to substantiate the reprisal allegation(s), even if the oversight investigator noted deficiencies in the investigation documentation. We estimate that DODIG sent the case back to the service IG for additional work in about 8 percent of service cases closed in fiscal year 2013. DODIG disagreed with the service determination of whether to substantiate the complaint, and took over the investigation, in 2 of the cases in our sample. DODIG officials stated that oversight investigators are in regular contact with the service IG headquarters to correct inadequacies in service investigations, but that these communications may not be documented in the case files.

During our case file review, we identified examples of DODIG oversight investigators not consistently completing the oversight worksheet. Specifically, from the results of our case file review, we estimate that for about 45 percent of service investigations closed in fiscal year 2013, DODIG oversight worksheets were missing narrative that indicated the investigator had thoroughly documented all case deficiencies or inconsistencies, as required on the oversight worksheet.[44] In those 45 percent of cases, we noted issues that include the following:

- *Case deficiencies were not consistently documented:* Some service investigation case files did not contain all DODIG required elements, such as required letters, interview transcripts or summaries, legal reviews, and other supporting documentation, but the oversight investigators did not note the missing documentation on the oversight worksheet.[45] Specifically, we estimate that in 19 percent of service investigated cases, the oversight investigator indicated that there were adequate transcripts or summaries of testimony; however, documentation of those interview transcripts was not included in the case file.

- *DODIG did not always note deficiencies that service IG headquarters identified:* We found instances in which DODIG investigators did not document deficiencies that the service IGs had identified. For example, a service IG-completed oversight worksheet, included in the investigation case file the service IG forwarded to DODIG for review, noted that the investigators did not appear fair and impartial in the servicemember interview transcript. In this interview transcript the investigator stated that in the military nothing is unbiased because there is a chain of command; however, DOD oversight investigators attested that the investigative file did not contain evidence of bias on the oversight worksheet. DODIG officials stated that there is no written requirement for oversight investigators to note deficiencies identified by the service IGs; however on oversight worksheets for other cases, the oversight investigators did note service IG-identified deficiencies. Service IG officials also highlighted inconsistencies between the oversight investigators. For example, service IG officials stated that they prefer to work with certain DODIG oversight investigators because they know what to expect from those oversight investigators, and this speeds up the oversight review. In contrast, these officials stated that they receive more questions about cases from oversight investigators with whom they work less frequently.
- *DODIG did not always explain why deficiencies did not affect the outcome of the service investigation:* In the instances when the DODIG oversight investigator identified deficiencies with the service IG investigation, the oversight investigator typically included a statement indicating that the noted deficiencies did not have a material effect on the outcome of the investigation. However, the oversight investigators did not always explain why the deficiencies did not affect the outcome of the investigation. For example, on some oversight worksheets that we reviewed, the oversight investigators noted that the service IG investigator did not analyze a protected communication or a personnel action as part of the investigation, but that these items did not affect the outcome of the investigation.

We also found that the files in these cases lacked documentation of the oversight investigators' analysis of the effect of noted deficiencies on the outcome of the investigation. Oversight investigators stated that when they note any deficiencies in investigations, they typically discuss those deficiencies with their supervisors in order to determine whether to approve the case. DODIG officials stated that there are several gray areas in reprisal investigations and that these types of discussions are common practice when DODIG is deciding whether to approve a case; however, we found in our case-file review that the results of these conversations are not always documented on the oversight worksheet. CIGIE standards state that reasonable steps should be taken to ensure that pertinent issues are sufficiently resolved and that the results of investigative activities should be accurately and completely documented in the case file.[46] Further, *Standards for Internal Control in the Federal Government* provide that internal control and all transactions and other significant events need to be clearly documented, and the documentation should be readily available for examination.[47] Ensuring that oversight investigators document the basis for their determinations regarding independent decision making enables reviewers to ensure that such determinations are appropriate.

Moreover, DODIG does not have detailed guidance that specifies the steps and documentation requirements of the DODIG oversight investigators' review of service reprisal investigations, and whether or how any noted investigation deficiencies would affect the outcome of the investigation. DODIG has focused on its October 2014 issuance of the updated *Guide to Investigating Military Whistleblower Reprisal and Restriction Complaints*, which details best practices for reprisal investigations, but does not specify the steps DODIG investigators are to follow when conducting oversight of service IG investigations. In addition, DODIG's Administrative Investigations manual includes a 5-page overview of oversight reviews. However, the manual is not specific to oversight reviews of military whistleblower reprisal investigations and encompasses investigations of senior officials, and does not state what deficiencies are substantive and would affect the outcome of the investigation.

Further, part one of DODIG's Administrative Investigations manual refers investigators to a forthcoming third portion of the manual for detailed guidance on conducting oversight of military whistleblower reprisal investigations, which has not been developed. However, as of January 2015, DODIG officials stated that they were no longer planning to issue the third part of the manual and that they plan to incorporate some additional oversight procedures into the existing manual. Officials did not provide details on what procedures they plan to incorporate or when they plan to make the changes. Without additional guidance for its oversight investigator team, which would help formalize the oversight process, DODIG will continue to face inconsistency in both its oversight documentation and its review of service IG investigation outcomes. CIGIE standards state that to facilitate due professional care, organizations should establish written investigative policies and procedures. The complexity of reprisal investigations paired with the decentralized service IG structure underscores the importance of clear and consistent oversight review procedures and documentation requirements to ensure consistency across the department and that each reprisal complaint receives due professional care.

Senior DODIG officials stated that DODIG's Administrative Investigations component is taking steps to implement quality-assurance processes and that these processes will help prepare the component for an eventual peer review. For example, a senior DODIG official said that on a quarterly basis, DODIG completes an internal control checklist for 20 DODIG whistleblower reprisal investigations and 20 oversight reviews of service IG military whistleblower reprisal investigations to assess the thoroughness of the case files and the completeness of the information in the case management system, among other things. This official also stated that they brief DODIG leadership on the results of these quarterly quality-assurance checks. The Whistleblower Reprisal Investigations directorate has undergone external reviews, but CIGIE has not established peer-review criteria for administrative investigations, such as whistleblower reprisal investigations, according to DODIG officials. Senior DODIG officials stated that, if established, they would like to participate in an eventual administrative peer review of their whistleblower reprisal investigations. However, without documentation of the steps it took to reach its case determinations and why any noted case deficiencies did not affect the outcome of the investigation, as well as consistent attestation of adherence to CIGIE standards, a third-party reviewer may find it difficult to assess the quality of DODIG's oversight process for military whistleblower reprisal investigations.

DODIG Does Not Have Standardized Investigative Guidance and Provides Limited Feedback on Investigation Quality

DODIG and the Service IGs Do Not Have Standardized Guidance Regarding Investigation Stages

DODIG and the service IGs use different terms in their guidance to refer to their investigation stages. DODIG took a step to improve guidance by issuing an updated reprisal investigation guide for military reprisal investigations for both DODIG and service IG investigators in October 2014.[48] The guide discusses DODIG's four questions that investigators use to determine whether the four elements of reprisal are present; various investigative steps; and, provides sample interview questions, among other things. However, DODIG describes the guide as best practices for conducting military reprisal intakes and investigations and, according to DODIG officials does not explicitly direct the services to follow DODIG's preferred investigation process and stages. DODIG officials stated that they have no role in the development of service IG regulations.

DODIG guidance describes two investigation stages: (1) intake and (2) full investigation. During the intake process, the investigator is to determine whether the servicemember made a protected communication and a responsible management official took a personnel action against the servicemember. In addition, if the investigator determines that the allegation supports an inference that the responsible management official had knowledge of the protected communication as well as a causal connection between the protected communication and the personnel action, and the servicemember reported the alleged reprisal within 1 year, the case is to proceed to a full investigation.[49] According to DODIG's investigation guide, during the intake process an investigator is to review the complaint, personnel action, and timeline; and interview the servicemember to clarify the allegation. During a full investigation, investigators are to formally interview the servicemember (and provide a written record of the interview), obtain relevant documentation (of the protected communication and personnel action, among other things), interview knowledgeable witnesses, interview the responsible management official who took the personnel action, and obtain a legal review of the report of investigation.

Each of the service IGs has a stage between intake and full investigation, commonly referred to as a preliminary inquiry or a reprisal complaint analysis. DODIG does not have a similar in-between investigation stage, and therefore DODIG officials stated that oversight investigators should classify preliminary inquiries conducted by the service IGs as intakes in the case management system, but there is no written guidance for reviewing preliminary inquiries. We found that the service investigators typically complete much more investigative work, such as interviewing witnesses, when conducting a preliminary inquiry than DODIG requires during the intake process.

Based on our case file review, we found that DODIG oversight investigators were not consistently classifying the preliminary inquiries as intakes, and classified many preliminary inquiries as full investigations in the case management system. DODIG oversight investigators approved cases as full investigations when those cases did not contain all elements required for full investigations and approved the dismissal of cases that were preliminary inquiries coded as full investigations, on a basis that can only be determined by conducting a full investigation. Specifically, we estimate that in 38 percent of preliminary inquiries closed in fiscal year 2013, service IGs dismissed cases because they determined that the responsible management official would have taken the personnel action absent the protected communication. In contrast, DODIG guidance states that an investigator answers the question of whether the responsible management official would have taken the personnel action absent the protected communication during a full investigation, which requires an interview with the responsible official to determine his or her reasons and motive for taking the personnel action.[50] In addition, a senior DODIG official stated that an investigator must interview the responsible management official to determine whether the personnel action would have occurred absent the protected communication. However, there was no evidence in these case files that the investigator interviewed the responsible management official, and instead, investigators determined that the responsible management officials took personnel actions as a result of the servicemembers' performance histories.

Further, we found through our file review that the service IGs' preliminary inquiry case files were less complete than the service IGs' full investigation case files, although DODIG oversight investigators approved preliminary inquiries as full investigations.[51] For example, based on our sample results, we estimate that at least 79 percent of service preliminary inquiries closed in fiscal year 2013 were missing at least one key element, such as interviews with the servicemember.[52] We estimate that at least 23 percent of service full investigations closed in fiscal year 2013 were missing at least one element.[53] Further, as previously discussed, DODIG's guidance requires investigators to interview the servicemember for all complaints, during the intake process and if the case proceeds to a full investigations; however, we estimate that 59 percent of service preliminary inquiry case files compared to 10 percent of service full investigation case files were missing evidence of a servicemember interview.[54]

CIGIE quality standards for investigations state that to facilitate due professional care, organizations should establish written investigative policies and procedures that are revised regularly according to evolving laws, regulations, and executive orders. [55] DODIG's investigation guide does not discuss preliminary inquiries or define any requirements for this stage of investigation. DODIG officials have stated that they would like the service IGs to stop preparing preliminary inquiries and to use DODIG's preferred investigation stages—intake and full investigation; however, DODIG guidance does not explicitly direct the services to use its preferred terms and stages. Additionally, a DODIG oversight investigator stated that the service IGs' varying interpretations of DOD policy and inconsistent application of DODIG guidance makes it difficult for oversight investigators to systematically review reprisal cases. The oversight investigator also stated that DODIG should explicitly direct the services to follow certain procedures currently included in DODIG guidance, but DODIG officials stated the office does not have a role in the development of service IG regulations. Further, in the absence of standardized investigation stages, DODIG investigators miscoded investigations in fiscal year 2013. We estimate that about 43 percent of the cases that DODIG closed in fiscal year 2013 that staff coded as full investigations were not fully investigated, and were instead preliminary inquiries as indicated in the service report of investigation. DODIG officials stated that this miscoding was likely the result of oversight investigators wanting to recognize the amount of work that service IG investigators completed, since those investigators typically complete the steps of a full investigation, except for an interview with the responsible management official and a legal review.

Without directing the service IGs to follow standardized investigation stages and issuing guidance clarifying how the stages are defined, it will be difficult for DODIG to ensure consistent program implementation. For example, the service IGs may do more investigative work than DODIG requires by conducting a preliminary inquiry, when DODIG would dismiss the case at intake. On the other hand, the service IGs may dismiss cases after conducting a preliminary inquiry when a DODIG investigator would conduct a full investigation and collect additional testimonial evidence. The amount of investigative work is inconsistent across DOD and is dependent on which IG investigates the complaint, which could lead to the perception that not all servicemember complaints are treated equally. In addition, without standardized investigation stages and corresponding guidance, investigators may be unclear about what elements are required for each stage of investigation, resulting in incomplete reprisal case files. Finally, without standardized investigative stages and agreement among DODIG oversight investigators about how to classify preliminary inquiries, DODIG may continue to miscode service preliminary inquiries in its case management system. Since this system is the basis for DODIG's semiannual reports to Congress, DODIG may mischaracterize the number of fully investigated complaints in these reports.

DODIG Does Not Consistently Provide Service IG Investigators with Feedback on Investigation Quality

DODIG has developed tools to assess service IG investigation quality and to note any case deficiencies, but DODIG does not consistently provide the service IGs with this feedback. As previously discussed, DODIG oversight investigators are to document their reviews of service IG investigations by completing an oversight worksheet. The worksheet contains the criteria against which the reports of investigation are to be evaluated to ensure that the investigations adhered to CIGIE professional standards, such as independence and thoroughness. The worksheet also includes spaces where the oversight investigator can include comments regarding any criteria the investigation did or did not meet.

According to DODIG's Administrative Investigations manual, which guides how DODIG investigators conduct and perform oversight of reprisal investigations, upon completion of the oversight review process, investigators are to provide the service IGs with copies of the oversight worksheet.[56] The manual further states that this affords a good mechanism for feedback to the services on the quality of individual cases, in addition to valuable information on trends in systemic deficiencies in investigations within their service. However, according to DODIG officials, in 2012 DODIG stopped providing the service IGs with completed oversight worksheets. Instead, these officials stated that they provide summarized feedback in the closure memorandums that they send to the service IGs once they approve a case. According to DODIG officials, the oversight investigators complete the oversight worksheet when reviewing service IG cases, but the worksheet is now used as an internal tool for review.

Service IG officials stated that the primary feedback they receive is DODIG's summarized case analysis on the closure memorandum, which discusses why it agreed with the service IG's determination; however, the closure memorandum, unlike the worksheet, does not include the criteria against which the investigations are assessed. Further, service IG officials stated that they upload DODIG's closure memorandums to their respective case management system, but they do not require the investigating officers to go into the case management system to review the closure memorandum. A DODIG oversight investigator noted that the feedback oversight investigators provide on the worksheet is more constructive than what they include on the closure memorandum, and a service IG official stated that what investigators need is constructive feedback, not just statements about what they did not do correctly. A senior service IG official stated that receiving copies of the oversight worksheets was beneficial to service investigators because the worksheets helped investigators understand what DODIG was looking for in its reviews of service investigations. Additionally, according to service IG officials, DODIG rarely sends cases back to them for additional work and rarely asks questions regarding cases they have sent to DODIG for review. Service IG officials indicated that this lack of case-specific feedback from DODIG is confirmation to them that they are meeting DODIG's expectations for investigations; however, DODIG oversight investigators noted that the quality of service IG investigations could be improved. Further, through our review of cases closed in fiscal year 2013, after DODIG stopped providing copies of the oversight worksheets, we found examples where oversight investigators were providing case-specific feedback intended for the service IG investigators. For example, on some oversight worksheets the oversight investigator noted that the feedback provided on the worksheet was intended to be a teach-and-train vehicle to improve the quality and thoroughness of future reports; however, per DODIG's new practice, it is unclear whether DODIG provided these oversight worksheets to the service IG investigators.

DOD officials have noted that feedback to service IG investigators is important for various reasons. First, the DOD investigative process is decentralized and lacks continuity. Many offices at various levels of the service IGs investigate reprisal complaints. Further, in the Army and Air Force—which accounted for approximately 80 percent of the service investigative workload in fiscal years 2013 and 2014—military investigators typically rotate every 3 years, according to service IG officials. As such, these service IG military investigators may conduct few reprisal investigations and may not have the opportunity to develop experience, which according to DOD officials is essential to conducting high-quality reprisal investigations. The service IGs have taken steps to provide feedback to field-level investigators. For example, one service IG holds quarterly video-teleconferences with field-level investigators to share updates to reprisal policies and address any investigation trends. Second, according to service IG investigators, they receive some required training that is specific to conducting reprisal investigations when they are assigned to the IG, but there is no additional mandatory reprisal-specific training that investigators complete during the course of their careers. Additionally, these investigators may not have opportunities to apply lessons learned from that training immediately, and according to DOD officials there is often a gap of over a year between training and reprisal investigation assignment. According to CIGIE quality standards for investigations, organizations should establish appropriate avenues for investigators to acquire and maintain the necessary knowledge, skills, and abilities. Service IG investigators noted that in addition to offered training, case-specific feedback is a good way to learn skills for conducting reprisal investigations; however, three of six field-level investigators we interviewed stated that they had never received feedback from DODIG on their reprisal investigations.

If the service IG investigators do not receive copies of the oversight worksheet, they may not have knowledge of the criteria that DODIG uses to conduct its oversight reviews and whether their investigative reports are meeting the specific CIGIE standards that DODIG has incorporated into its oversight review. For example, three of six field-level investigators we interviewed had not seen a DODIG oversight worksheet, and two of those three investigators did not know that DODIG used a worksheet to conduct oversight. DODIG's October 2014 guide for investigating reprisal complaints includes a quality-assurance review checklist, modeled after the DODIG oversight review worksheet, that investigators can use to perform a quality-assurance review of their investigation. However, as previously discussed, service IG investigators are not subject to or consistently trained to CIGIE standards and therefore may not know how to assess their investigations according to these standards.[57] Without receiving case-specific feedback, which relates to the CIGIE standards against which DODIG assessed the investigation and notes any deficiencies, service investigators may not be able to assess their own subsequent investigations. Further, without coordination with the service IGs to ensure that service investigators are receiving case-specific feedback from DODIG, DODIG efforts to improve investigation quality may continue to face challenges. Finally, without case-specific feedback, service IGs may not be able to identify trends in systematic deficiencies or specific CIGIE standards not being met, which otherwise might be corrected in future investigations and incorporated into their feedback to field-level investigators.

DOD Does Not Have a Process for Investigators to Certify Their Independence

DODIG and the service IGs have processes for investigators to recuse themselves from investigations, but there is no process for investigators to document whether the investigation they conducted was independent and outside of the chain of command. CIGIE standards state that in all matters relating to investigative work, the investigative organization must be free, both in fact and appearance, from impairments to independence. Impairments to independence include professional or personal relationships that might weaken the investigative work in any way, and preconceived opinions of individuals or groups that could bias the investigation, among others.

In the absence of a process for investigators to certify their independence, DODIG has incorporated various questions into its oversight review in order to document the independence of the investigator and to determine whether the investigation was conducted in accordance with CIGIE standards. For example, DODIG oversight investigators indicate whether the investigator was outside the chain of command of the servicemember and responsible management official, which is statutorily required. DODIG's oversight investigators—of which all but one has prior military experience—stated that they use their experience and knowledge of the service's organizational structures to determine whether the investigator was outside the chain of command. Oversight investigators further determine on the current version of the oversight worksheet whether the investigator maintained professionalism and demonstrated IG impartiality during interviews. Oversight investigators stated that they can determine whether the investigator was impartial during interviews only if the case has interview transcripts, which the Administrative Investigations Manual instructs them to read if necessary; however, DODIG will accept summarized interviews and does not require that the service IGs provide verbatim transcripts for all interviews. Based on our sample, we estimate that 43 percent of cases closed in fiscal year 2013 have transcripts of interviews with the servicemember alleging reprisal and 26 percent of cases have transcripts of responsible management official interviews. In the absence of interview transcripts, oversight investigators have limited tools to determine whether the investigator demonstrated IG impartiality during interviews.

DOD officials stated that their recusal policies and decentralized investigation structure, removing the investigator from the chain of command, adequately address independence and that no further documentation of independence is needed. However, during our case-file review we reviewed oversight worksheets where DODIG oversight investigators had noted potential impairments to investigator objectivity in the report of investigation. For example, on one oversight worksheet, the oversight investigator stated that the report gave the appearance of service investigator bias, and further clarified that the report should state whether the responsible management official's actions were reasonable and supported by facts, not whether the investigator would have taken the same actions. In addition, on another oversight worksheet the DODIG investigator stated that the investigator's narrative in the report of investigation contained comments that would bring into question whether the analysis was impartial and unbiased, further noting that there was evidence of bias. Further, one oversight worksheet stated that the investigator was not outside the chain of command, as statutorily required, but that it had no effect on the investigation. DODIG approved these cases without documenting how it reconciled these case deficiencies. We are not questioning DODIG's judgment in these cases.

We noted that the files in these cases did not address the issues identified by the oversight investigator beyond the final approval of the case. However, *Standards for Internal Control in the Federal Government* provides that internal control and all transactions and other significant events need to be clearly documented, and the documentation should be readily available for examination. Without documenting the basis for their determinations regarding independent decision making, DODIG cannot ensure that such determinations are appropriate.

One oversight investigator we interviewed stated that DODIG has received investigations from the service IGs where the investigations show clear signs of bias, even though the investigator was outside the chain of command. According to this investigator, in these instances, DODIG's options include returning the case for additional investigation, appointing a new investigator, or preparing additional case analysis addressing the bias. Further, some service IG reviews of investigations also noted potential impairments to objectivity. For example, a service IG forwarded a completed investigation to DODIG for approval, noting that the investigators did not appear fair and impartial in a servicemember interview transcript; however, the oversight investigator stated that there was no evidence of bias by the investigating officer. Service IG officials stated that their review of field-level investigations is important because they have received investigations that contain personal opinion and statements that make it appear that the investigator was not impartial. These officials stated that, through their review, they attempt to identify and correct these statements, and that DODIG's subsequent review of the case should also catch any instances where an investigator did not appear impartial. Service IG officials noted that, because investigators are so close to the investigation, they can become invested in the investigation and that this investment is sometimes evident in reports of investigation.

Guidance for documenting independence is included in generally accepted government auditing standards (GAGAS).[58] While these standards apply to audits, they can also provide guidance to service IGs as a best practice on how to document decisions regarding independence when conducting reprisal investigations. Documentation of independence considerations provides evidence of the judgments in forming conclusions regarding compliance with independence requirements. Further, GAGAS notes that an organization should establish policies and procedures in its system of quality control that address independence. While GAGAS states that insufficient documentation of compliance with the independence standard does not impair independence, documentation of independence in a reprisal investigation could improve the quality of DODIG's investigations. Without a process for investigators to document that the investigation was independent and outside the chain of command, DODIG and the service IGs will be hindered in their efforts to monitor the independence of investigations. DODIG oversight investigators are responsible for assessing the independence of the investigator and the investigation. Absent direction from DODIG to the service IGs to provide certifications that the investigator was independent and outside of the chain of command, DODIG oversight investigators have few mechanisms to determine whether the investigation was independent during the oversight process. With the pending expansion of DODIG's case management system to the service IGs, the certification process could be incorporated, for example, into the case management system. Further, such a certification process would serve as an accountability mechanism for service IG investigators, should an oversight investigator or service IG official note any potential impairments to objectivity during their reviews of investigations. Finally, certification of investigator independence could decrease the potential for bias in military reprisal investigations and better ensure that servicemembers receive the whistleblower protections provided by law.

CONCLUSION

Whistleblowers play an important role in safeguarding the federal government against waste, fraud, and abuse, and their willingness to come forward can contribute to improvements in government operations. As a result, it is important that DOD have a process for investigating whistleblower reprisal complaints that affected parties have confidence is timely, effective, and impartial. One way in which such confidence can be undermined is if investigations and related communications with the servicemembers are not timely and accurate. Reducing delays in investigations and notifications when the process will take longer than 180 days would provide servicemembers with information that may affect their immediate work environment or personnel actions, which are typically halted during an active investigation, since servicemembers generally do not receive relief from reprisal until DODIG has approved a substantiated investigation. Ultimately, the absence of regular status updates, such as revised case-completion estimates when time frames shift, may discourage servicemembers from coming forward to report wrongdoing.

Another area in which DODIG processes are lacking is in data collection and monitoring for oversight of investigations at the service IG level. DODIG has made progress in this regard since our February 2012 report by implementing a new case management system, but it remains under development and, as of March 2015, does not yet meet DODIG's full reporting needs. Without additional internal guidance to staff on how to use the case management system for real-time case processing, DODIG cannot assure efficient reporting and that the data it collects are up to date and accurate. Absent these actions, along with developing an implementation plan for expansion of the case management system to the service IGs, DODIG will not have complete visibility of service IG workload and timeliness.

DODIG also cannot ensure that all military whistleblower reprisal investigations adhere to quality standards. For instance, the complexity of reprisal investigations underscores the need for clear and consistent oversight review procedures and documentation requirements. DODIG took a positive step by establishing a team of investigators that is solely dedicated to the review of service IG investigations. However, without additional guidance regarding how to review service IG investigations, which would help to formalize the oversight process, DODIG cannot ensure that it treats reprisal complaints consistently and with due professional care. In addition, consistency across DODIG and service IG investigations, especially in regard to investigation stages, will be limited without guidance that clarifies the amount of investigative work an investigator is to conduct at each stage and leads to the perception that not all servicemember complaints are treated equally. Additionally, without providing case-specific feedback that includes the criteria DODIG oversight investigators use to assess service investigations, service investigators may be limited in their ability to improve the quality of subsequent investigations. Finally, DOD may not be able to enhance the perception of fairness and increase accountability without taking steps to develop and implement a process for investigators to certify their independence when conducting investigations. Absent these actions, DODIG will be limited in its ability to enhance the effectiveness of its oversight, prepare for the eventual peer review in which senior leadership would like to participate, and ensure that servicemembers receive the whistleblower protections provided by law.

RECOMMENDATIONS FOR EXECUTIVE ACTION

To improve the military whistleblower reprisal investigation process and oversight of such investigations, we recommend that the Secretary of Defense work in coordination with the Department of Defense Inspector General (DODIG) to take the following seven actions:

- develop an automated tool to help ensure compliance with the statutory 180-day notification requirement by providing servicemembers with accurate information regarding the status of their reprisal investigations within 180 days of receipt of an allegation of reprisal;
- issue additional guidance to investigators on how to use the case management system as a real-time management tool, and update and finalize the draft internal user guidance from 2012 as necessary until the case management system is complete;
- working in coordination with the service IGs, develop an implementation plan that addresses the needs of DODIG and the service IGs, and defines project goals, schedules, costs, stakeholder roles and responsibilities, and stakeholder communication techniques for expansion of the case management system;
- issue additional guidance to formalize the DODIG oversight process;
- direct the services to follow standardized investigation stages and issue guidance clarifying how the stages are defined;
- ensure that the mechanism it uses for feedback to service investigators includes the criteria against which the investigation was assessed and any deficiencies, and work with the service IG headquarters to ensure that feedback is shared with the service investigators; and
- develop and implement a process for investigators to document whether the investigation was independent and outside of the chain of command and direct the service IGs to provide such documentation for review during the oversight process.

Agency Comments and Our Evaluation

In commenting on a draft of this report, DODIG concurred with each of our seven recommendations. However, DODIG did not agree with the manner in which we presented the findings in the report and raised concerns that we did not include information relating to significant progress made by DODIG since our February 2012 report. DODIG also provided technical comments, which we considered and incorporated where appropriate.

We disagree with DODIG's characterization of our report's findings because we included discussion of the improvements cited by DODIG throughout our report. For example, we noted increases in staff levels, DODIG's development of a new case management system, DODIG's October 2014 issuance of a military whistleblower reprisal investigations guide, and policy guidance to the service IGs regarding 180-day notification requirements, among others. Further, in its comments, DODIG stated that it takes its role in leading DOD's whistleblower protection program seriously and has invested significant resources, more so than other federal agencies, to improve the timeliness and quality of its investigations. In addition, DODIG highlighted the volume of complaints that it processes. We agree that DOD's program is large, and believe that our current recommendations are critical to aid DODIG in attaining its goal of being the model whistleblower protection program in the federal government. Our responses to additional comments made by DODIG on our report's findings are included at the end of appendix III.

In concurring with our first recommendation that DODIG develop an automated tool to help ensure DOD compliance with the statutory 180- day notification requirement, DODIG stated it had already implemented a dashboard in its case management system that identifies investigations pending for 180 days and that it would work toward an even more automated notification process in the future. We believe that an automated tool to help ensure DOD compliance with statutory requirements is needed and that the dashboard alone does not serve this intended purpose. Based on our case file review, we found that in the estimated 53 percent of cases in which DOD sent the required 180-day notification letters for cases closed in fiscal year 2013, the notifications that DOD provided were sent after 180 days. Specifically, we estimated that DOD's median notification time was on average 353 days after the servicemember filed the complaint, almost twice as long as the 180-day requirement. The dashboard that DODIG uses to track cases does not proactively alert DOD to send the 180-day letter. Importantly, as we stated in our report, DODIG's case management system did not have record of at least 22 percent of service investigations both open as of September 30, 2014, and closed in fiscal years 2013 and 2014. Without knowledge of these cases, DODIG cannot ensure that the service IGs sent 180-day notification letters for cases taking over 180 days to complete. We believe that an automated tool that proactively alerts DOD to send the required 180-day notification letter for all cases taking longer than 180 day days could help to ensure DOD's full compliance with statutory notification requirements.

In concurring with our second recommendation that DODIG issue additional guidance to investigators on how to use the case management system as a real-time management tool, DODIG stated that we misrepresented DODIG's focused effort to migrate paper-based 2013 data into a new electronic system and correct data deficiencies in order to ensure data reliability. We disagree. In our report, we note that DODIG officials told us that the case management system is to serve as a real-time complaint tracking and investigative management tool for investigators. Further, in its comments, DODIG highlights the guidance and training it has implemented related to its case management system. During our case file review, we found that personnel uploaded key case documents to the case management system after DODIG had closed the case in 77 percent of cases closed in fiscal year 2013 and made changes to case variables in 83 percent of cases in 2014. DODIG staff made these changes at least 3 months after case closure and at least a year after DODIG implemented the database in December 2012, indicating that it was not being used for real-time case tracking for cases closed in fiscal year 2013. Further, despite DODIG's stated efforts to train investigators and ensure data consistency, we found significant instances of coding errors where DODIG personnel were coding partially completed service investigations as full investigations. Specifically, we estimate that for cases closed in fiscal year 2013, 43 percent of cases that DODIG investigators coded as fully investigated were only partially investigated. As a result, we believe that additional guidance on how to use the case management system may help ensure that DODIG has awareness of the real-time status of cases and the reliability of DODIG's data.

In concurring with our third recommendation that DODIG work in coordination with the service IGs to develop an implementation plan for the expansion of the case management system, DODIG stated that we did not acknowledge the steps it has already taken to develop an implementation plan. We disagree. As we note in the report, DODIG officials stated during our review that they were developing an implementation strategy for the expansion of the case management system, but that they did not have an implementation plan. DODIG stated that it has taken additional actions since January 2015 to plan for the expansion of the case management system, such as developing a demonstration environment to define the requirement gaps. We believe that these actions are positive steps and that they will provide a strong foundation for the development of an implementation plan, which could help position DODIG to monitor the case management system expansion and measure project success.

In concurring with our fourth recommendation that DODIG issue additional guidance to formalize the DODIG oversight process, DODIG stated that its investigations manual already provides formal guidance to DODIG investigators for conducting oversight reviews of service IG military reprisal investigations and that within the next 90 days it will develop additional guidance on conducting oversight reviews, such as how to evaluate and document deficiencies, including those that did not affect the overall outcome of the investigation. We disagree that DODIG's investigations manual already provides formal oversight guidance. We reviewed the 5-page chapter in DODIG's manual on oversight of service IG investigations, and we found that it does not detail the steps and documentation requirements of an oversight review, is not specific to military whistleblower reprisal investigations, and does not state what deficiencies are substantive and would affect the outcome of an investigation. We believe that DODIG's stated plan to develop additional guidance, including how to evaluate and document deficiencies, could better ensure the consistency of DODIG's oversight reviews and that all reprisal complaints receive due professional care.

In concurring with our fifth recommendation that DODIG direct the services to follow standardized investigation stages and issue guidance clarifying how the stages are defined, DODIG stated that its October 2014 military whistleblower reprisal investigations guide describes DODIG's intake process and that its Directive 7050.06, which was reissued in April 2015, establishes a timeline for completing the intake process in 30 days. We disagree that the guidance provides the needed instructions for investigators. We acknowledged in the report that DOD's issuance of updated guidance is a positive step; however, DODIG describes its guide as a best practice for conducting military reprisal intakes and investigations and does not explicitly direct the services to follow DODIG's preferred stages. In addition, it does not discuss the service IGs' use of preliminary inquiries to dismiss cases after only a partial investigation, a practice DODIG stated it ended 3 years ago. We believe that standardized investigative stages may better ensure consistent program implementation and that all servicemember complaints are treated equally.

In concurring with our sixth recommendation that DODIG ensure that feedback to service investigators includes the criteria against which the investigation was assessed and any deficiencies, and that feedback is shared with the service investigators, DODIG stated that within the next 60 days it will resume its prior practice of sending oversight worksheets to the service IGs. Those worksheets will include the criteria against which the service's intake or investigation was reviewed as well as clear explanations of deficiencies and whether they affected the outcome of the case. DODIG also stated that it will work with the services to develop a mechanism by which results will be shared with service investigators. We believe that the steps DODIG noted in its response could improve the quality of future service IG investigations and better ensure that investigative reports meet the CIGIE standards that DODIG has incorporated into its oversight review.

In concurring with our seventh recommendation that DODIG develop and implement a process for investigators to document whether the investigation was independent and outside of the chain of command, DODIG stated that within the next 60 days it will develop and implement such a process. Specifically, it stated that the process will require service investigators to attest in writing that they are outside the immediate chain of command of both the servicemember alleging reprisal and the alleged responsible management officials. Although such an attestation is a positive step, we believe that the service investigators should also attest to whether the investigation was independent. DODIG oversight worksheets we reviewed noted impairments to investigator objectivity in reports of investigation even though the service investigator was outside of the chain of command. We believe that an attestation that the investigation is both independent and outside of the chain of command could help serve as an accountability mechanism for service IG investigators and decrease the potential for bias in military whistleblower reprisal investigations.

Brenda S. Farrell
Director
Defense Capabilities and Management

APPENDIX I: SCOPE AND METHODOLOGY

To address our objectives, we used two primary sources of data, including (1) closed military whistleblower reprisal case data from the Department of Defense Office of Inspector General's (DODIG) case management system and (2) a randomly selected sample of DODIG's closed military whistleblower reprisal case files. DODIG provided us with information for all military whistleblower reprisal cases closed from October 1, 2011, through September 30, 2014, and all cases open as of October 1, 2014. We were unable to report the fiscal year 2012 data because DODIG transitioned to a new case management system in December 2012, and data from fiscal year 2012 were not reliable as a result of the data migration, according to DODIG officials. In addition, DODIG officials told us that they verified and corrected data as necessary for all cases closed in fiscal years 2013 and 2014 because the case management system was new and investigators had not been consistently recording information. We assessed the reliability of DODIG's fiscal years 2013 and 2014 data—by reviewing related documentation, interviewing knowledgeable officials, and comparing selected fields, such as open and closed dates, with case file records from our sample—and concluded that the data were sufficiently reliable for reporting the average lengths of investigations.

Further, we used the data for cases closed in fiscal year 2013 to select the sample for our case-file review, discussed below. We chose cases from this period for the file review because of DODIG's case management system transition in December 2012 and statements from DODIG officials that data from cases closed in the old case management system were not as complete as data from cases closed in the new case management system. We also chose this period because the National Defense Authorization Act for Fiscal Year 2014, effective December 26, 2013, expanded the amount of time a servicemember has to report a reprisal allegation from 60 days to 365 days. We selected a stratified random sample of 135 cases from the 538 cases closed in fiscal year 2013. We stratified the population into six strata by combining three categories of case status and two categories of investigation status (see table 5 below). We calculated the sample sizes to achieve a desired precision of plus or minus 10 percentage points or fewer for a percentage estimate of the total population (N=538) at the 95 percent confidence level. We then adjusted the sample sizes to achieve a desired precision of plus or minus 10 percentage points or fewer for a percentage estimate at the 95 percent confidence level for

DODIG Oversight cases (N=344, strata 3 and 4) and Fully Investigated cases (N=203, strata 1, 3, and 5).

Table 5. Description of Stratification and Population and Sample Sizes

Stratum (Case status / investigation status)	Population size	Sample size
1. Intake Dismissed : Fully Investigated	1	1
2. Intake Dismissed : Not Fully Investigated	172	27
3. Oversight : Fully Investigated	183	59
4. Oversight : Not Fully Investigated	161	36
5. Other: Fully Investigated	19	10
6. Other: Not Fully Investigated	2	2
Total	538	135

Source: GAO analysis of Department of Defense Inspector General (DODIG) data. | GAO-15-477

During the course of our review, we removed 11 out-of-scope cases, which reduced the original sample size from 135 to 124, because we found that 2 of the cases were open, 1 of the cases was classified and had limited documentation to review, and 8 cases were investigations of improper mental health examinations and not reprisal. This reduced sample of 124 cases is generalizable to the estimated population of in-scope cases. We generalized the results of our sample to the estimated population of 498 cases DODIG closed in fiscal year 2013. All estimates of percentages presented in this report have a margin of error of plus or minus 10 percentage points or fewer, unless otherwise noted. Further, all estimates of medians and averages presented in this report have a relative error of plus or minus 20 percent of the estimate, unless otherwise noted.

To determine the extent to which the Department of Defense (DOD) has met statutory notification requirements and internal timeliness requirements for completing military whistleblower reprisal investigations, we calculated the timeliness of cases using case data from DODIG's case management system for military whistleblower reprisal cases closed in fiscal years 2013 and 2014 and compared the average timeliness to the regulatory 180-day requirement. We removed one closed case from the timeliness calculations because the record produced a negative case processing time because the closed date preceded the open date. In addition, for all cases that were open as of September 30, 2014, we analyzed how long the cases had been open, according to the fiscal year in which the complaints were received. To determine the extent to which DOD met the statutory requirement to notify servicemembers in cases lasting longer than 180 days about delays in the investigation in fiscal year 2013, we reviewed the 124 case files in our sample for evidence that DOD had sent the required letter in cases lasting longer than 180 days. For cases where there was evidence that DOD had sent the required letter, we recorded the reasons provided for the delay as well as the estimated completion date. We calculated the median estimated time frame in the letters and compared this to the median completion date for these cases to determine the accuracy of DOD's estimated time frames. In order to assess the reliability of DODIG's data, we used case file documentation to determine the open and close dates of the 124 cases in our sample and calculated total case time for each case. We then compared the total case time we recorded for the sample cases to the total case time for those cases in DODIG's data and we found a mean difference of 2 days. We further assessed the data through discussions with officials responsible for the data and concluded that the data were sufficiently reliable for reporting the average lengths of investigations. Further, we reviewed relevant documents including 10 U.S.C. § 1034, as amended, and its implementing directive on military whistleblower protections, DOD Directive 7050.06, *Military Whistleblower Protection* (July 23, 2007). After we sent our draft report for comment, DODIG issued an updated Directive on April 17, 2015, which we also reviewed. Finally, we interviewed officials about methods for tracking investigations and processes for sending required notifications to servicemembers that allege reprisal. We also collected relevant documentation, such as standard operating procedures and investigative guidance from DODIG, and the service Inspectors General (IG) for the Air Force, the Army, the Marine Corps and the Navy. We also spoke with officials from DODIG's Information Systems directorate to determine which variables to request from DODIG's case management system.

To determine the extent to which DODIG's whistleblower case management system supports oversight of the military whistleblower reprisal program, we obtained and analyzed closed case data from each of the service IGs for cases closed from fiscal year 2012 through fiscal year 2014. We assessed the reliability of service IG data from fiscal years 2013 and 2014—by reviewing related documentation and interviewing knowledgeable officials—and concluded that the data were sufficiently reliable for our purposes. We compared selected variables for all cases by matching DODIG's data to the service IG data to identify duplicate cases and missing information, and to determine whether DODIG has visibility of all ongoing and closed military whistleblower reprisal cases. We selected the variables present in both DODIG's and the service IGs' data to compare for matching cases in consultation with DODIG and service officials, and those variables include servicemember name, case identifiers, open date, and closed date. Further, we interviewed DODIG officials responsible for the development of the case management system and the proposed expansion of the case management system to the service IGs and collected supporting documentation. We also reviewed DOD memorandums regarding the case management system expansion and cost information for the next phase of case management system development and compared these documents to relevant program management criteria. In addition, we interviewed officials from DODIG's Administrative Investigations component as well as its Whistleblower Reprisal Investigations and Investigations of Senior Officials directorates, and service IG officials regarding the case management system expansion.

To determine the extent to which DOD has processes to ensure oversight of military whistleblower reprisal investigations conducted by the service IGs, we used our stratified random sample of 124 case files retained by DODIG for military whistleblower reprisal cases that DODIG closed from October 1, 2012, through September 30, 2013. Based on our review of whistleblower reprisal investigation policies and procedures and quality standards for investigations established by the Council of the Inspectors General on Integrity and Efficiency (CIGIE), we created a data-collection instrument to identify the key characteristics of whistleblower reprisal cases, determine the reliability of various fields in the case management system, and assess the completeness and quality of files.[1] We also developed a standard approach to electronically review files, using DODIG's new case management system, to ensure we reviewed all cases consistently. For example, for all cases, we reviewed the original complaint followed by the report of investigation and interview transcripts, among other things. We refined this data-collection instrument and our approach by first reviewing 12 pilot case files selected by DODIG that were not part of the 135 originally identified in the sample. Specifically, the pilot consisted of cases that DODIG approved in the first three quarters of fiscal year 2014, including 3 cases investigated by DODIG, 3 cases investigated by the Army, 2 cases investigated by the Air Force, 2 cases investigated by the Navy, and 2 cases investigated by the Marine Corps. Of those 12 cases, 11 were fully investigated and 6 were substantiated.

After the pilot, our methodology for reviewing the randomly sampled cases required each case to be reviewed first by one analyst and then reviewed by a second analyst who noted any disagreement with the first analyst's assessment. Analysts discussed the areas of disagreement and resolved any disagreement by identifying and reviewing supporting documentation in the case files. Further, two GAO investigators with professional investigative experience reviewed a portion of the sample and concurred with the analysts' assessment of the cases, in accordance with CIGIE guidelines for quality-assurance reviews. We did not question DODIG's judgment in these cases.

To assess case-file completeness, we reviewed DODIG's process, 10 U.S.C. § 1034, directive, and other guidance and consulted with DODIG officials and identified 13 elements to include in our case-file review. These 13 elements support the conclusions reached in the case, indicate compliance with the law or directive, or manage the internal communication not specifically outlined by law or directive. The 13 elements we included for our case file review are the following:

1) notification to DODIG from the service IG that received the complaint,
2) evidence supporting the recommended outcome,
3) investigation plan,
4) report of investigation or other written product,
5) legal review,
6) interview with servicemember,
7) interview with responsible management official,
8) DODIG oversight worksheet,
9) correspondence between DODIG and the servicemember regarding investigations taking longer than 180 days,
10) correspondence between DODIG and the Secretary of Defense regarding investigations taking longer than 180 days,
11) record of corrective action taken,
12) correspondence between DODIG and the service IGs regarding the final case outcome, and
13) correspondence between DOD and the servicemember regarding the final outcome of the case.

Some of these elements included specific documents. For example, the DODIG oversight worksheet (item 8 above) was a specific document. Other elements could be reflected in multiple documents. For example, the evidence supporting the recommended outcome (item 2 above) could be in a larger report, be in a summary, or be its own document. We determined the completeness of each case file selected in our sample individually since not all

13 elements were necessary in every case. For example, some of the 13 elements would only need to be present in a file if an investigation was conducted by a service IG or was a full investigation. We adjusted the required number of elements based on the specific circumstances of each case and calculated completeness based on that adjusted baseline. We categorized the case files by the average number of elements missing for each type of case, dismissed DODIG intakes, service IG preliminary inquiries, service IG full investigations, and DODIG full investigations.

We also interviewed investigators and supervisors on DODIG's oversight team and officials at each of the service headquarters IGs. In addition, we interviewed six field-level investigators from the Army, the Navy, and the Air Force IGs regarding required training, available guidance, and investigative processes, including assessing independence. We used data provided by each of the services for cases closed in fiscal year 2014 to select investigators for interviews. We used a simple random sampling technique to select investigators for interviews. We selected 12 investigators from the 216 investigations closed by the Army, 10 investigators from the 35 investigations closed by the Navy, and 10 investigators from the 110 investigations closed by the Air Force. Since field-level service IG investigators typically rotate every 2 to 3 years, we were able to contact and speak with two investigators from each service IG. In addition, we reviewed training materials, guidance, and requirements for investigators from DODIG and each of the service IGs as well as their processes for assessing investigator independence. We also attended training sessions related to conducting military whistleblower reprisal investigations at DODIG and the Army IG as well as 2 DODIG Administrative Investigations training symposia, which contained sessions on whistleblower reprisal investigations, and interviewed an official from CIGIE's Advanced Training Institute. Additionally, we compared DOD's independence processes to CIGIE quality standards for investigations and Generally Accepted Government Auditing Standards (GAGAS).

We conducted this performance audit from April 2014 to May 2015 in accordance with generally accepted government auditing standards. Those standards require that we plan and perform the audit to obtain sufficient, appropriate evidence to provide a reasonable basis for our findings and conclusions based on our audit objectives. We believe that the evidence obtained provides a reasonable basis for our findings and conclusions based on our audit objectives.

APPENDIX II: GENERAL INFORMATION ON CASE CHARACTERISTICS FOR MILITARY WHISTLEBLOWER REPRISAL INVESTIGATIONS

This appendix provides information on the characteristics of military whistleblower reprisal cases based on our case file review of 124 cases closed from October 1, 2012, through September 30, 2013, as well as data from the Department of Defense Office of Inspector General's (DODIG) case management system for cases closed in fiscal years 2013 and 2014.

Servicemember Characteristics for Closed Cases

Generally, the service affiliations of the servicemembers that alleged reprisal did not match the overall proportions in the military population. See figure 3 for a comparison of the servicemember population proportion by service compared to the proportion of reprisal cases closed.

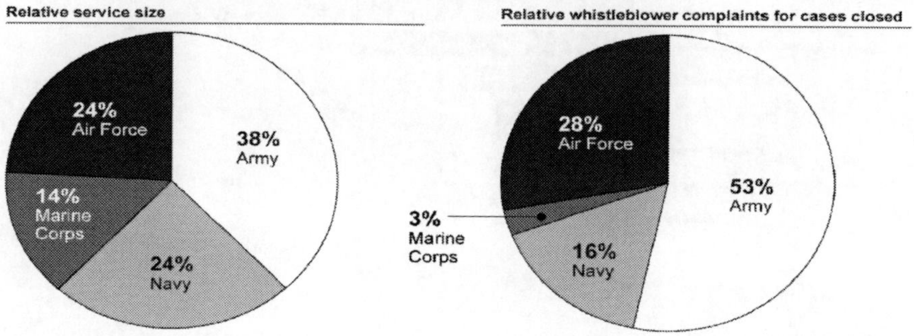

Source: GAO analysis of Department of Defense Inspector General (DODIG) data. | GAO-15-477.

Note: Forty complaint records in DODIG's case management system did not specify the servicemember's service affiliation, and those records were dropped from this analysis.

Figure 3. Relative Service Size versus Percentage of Military Whistleblower Complaints by Service for Cases Closed in Fiscal Years 2013 and 2014.

Through our file review of cases closed in fiscal year 2013, we estimate that the majority of servicemembers filed reprisal complaints with a service Inspector General (IG) (70 percent). Servicemembers also filed reprisal complaints with the DODIG Hotline (23 percent) and through Members of Congress (6 percent).

Protected Communication Characteristics

According to Department of Defense (DOD) Directive 7050.06, a servicemember who makes or prepares to make a protected communication is a whistleblower. Based on our review of case files closed in 2013, we estimate that the primary reasons for making a protected communication are to report allegations of a violation of law or regulation (49 percent), abuse of authority (39 percent), or a general communication to the IG (23 percent). Other reasons for making a protected communication included funds or resource waste (14 percent), public health or safety danger (11 percent,) and sexual assault (8 percent), among others.[1]

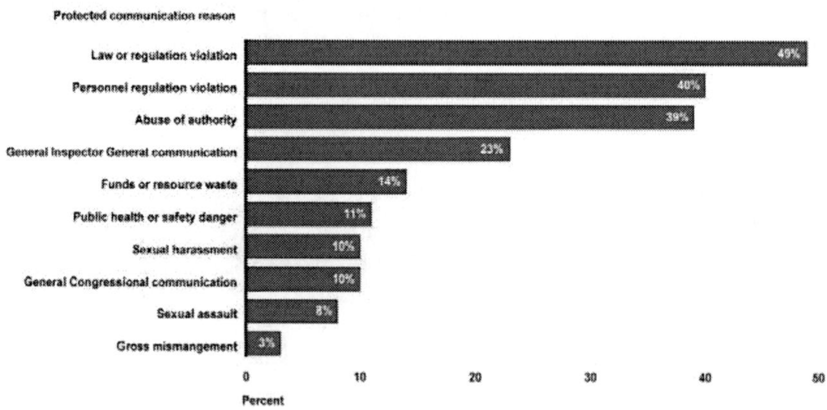

Source: GAO analysis of Department of Defense Inspector General (DODIG) data. | GAO-15-477.

Note: Percentages do not add up to 100 percent because servicemembers can make multiple protected communications. All percentage estimates in this figure have a margin of error of plus or minus 10 percentage points or fewer at the 95 percent confidence level.

Figure 4. Estimated Percentage of Protected Communication Reasons for Military Whistleblower Cases Closed in Fiscal Year 2013.

DOD officials told us that regulations cover virtually every aspect of military life, including how to conduct personnel ratings, so servicemembers often cite violations of regulations in their complaints. About 40 percent of cases in our sample included a protected communication regarding a personnel regulation violation. Figure 4 shows the reasons servicemembers made protected communications by frequency.

Further, based on our case file review, we estimate that the primary authorized recipients of protected communications for cases closed in fiscal year 2013 were the chain of command (62 percent), Inspectors General (53 percent), and Members of Congress (18 percent). DOD officials told us that the inclusion of the chain of command in the list of authorized protected communication recipients has resulted in an increase in the number of servicemembers that qualify as whistleblowers because reporting issues to the chain of command is a standard military procedure. Figure 5 shows the authorized recipients to whom servicemembers made protected communications by frequency.

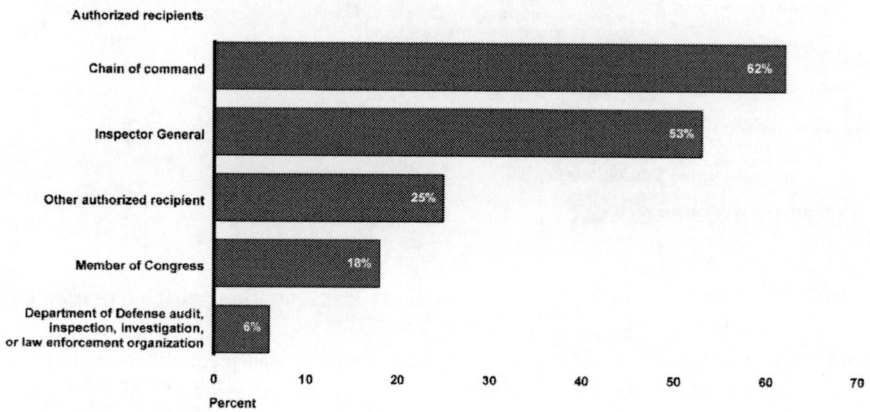

Source: GAO analysis of Department of Defense Inspector General (DODIG) data. | GAO-15-477.

Note: Percentages do not add up to 100 percent because servicemembers can make multiple protected communications to different authorized recipients. All percentage estimates in this figure have a margin of error of plus or minus 10 percentage points or fewer at the 95 percent confidence level.

Figure 5. Estimated Percentage of Protected Communications Made to Authorized Recipients for Military Whistleblower Cases Closed in Fiscal Year 2013.

Unfavorable Personnel Action Characteristics

A whistleblower reprisal complaint must also include an allegation that an action was taken in reprisal against a servicemember. DOD Directive 7050.06 defines reprisal as taking or threatening to take an unfavorable personnel action, or withholding or threatening to withhold a favorable personnel action, for making or preparing to make a protected communication.[2] Based on our file review of cases closed in fiscal year 2013, we estimate that the most common forms of reprisal alleged by servicemembers were that they received a poor performance evaluation (44 percent), disciplinary action (39 percent), or an unfavorable assignment or reassignment (27 percent). Figure 6 shows the frequency of the various types of personnel actions.

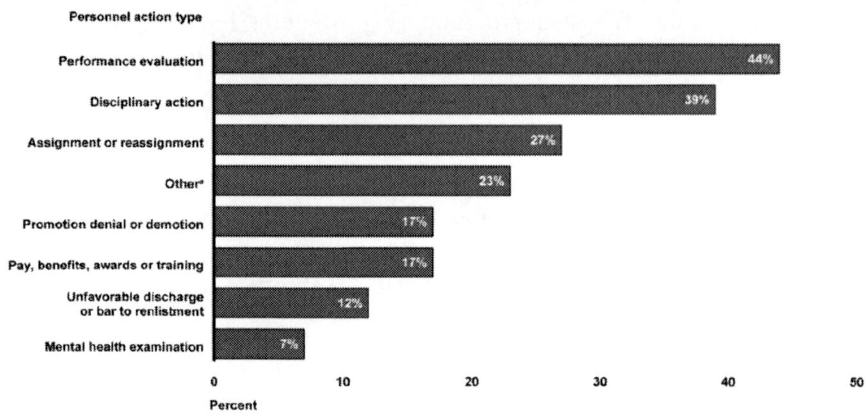

Source: GAO analysis of Department of Defense Inspector General (DODIG) data. | GAO-15-477.

Note: Percentages do not add up to 100 percent because servicemembers can allege multiple unfavorable personnel actions. All percentage estimates in this figure have a margin of error of plus or minus 10 percentage points or fewer at the 95 percent confidence level.

[a]Examples of other unfavorable personnel actions include restriction and responsible official initiating actions to revoke a security clearance, among other things.

Figure 6. Estimated Percentage of Unfavorable Personnel Action Types for Military Whistleblower Cases Closed in Fiscal Year 2013.

Reasons for Closing Cases

DODIG evaluates cases and generally closes them based on the answers to four questions, which investigators use to determine whether a case has all of the elements of reprisal. Specifically:

1) Did the servicemember make or prepare to make a protected communication, or was the servicemember perceived as having made or prepared to make a protected communication?
2) Was an unfavorable personnel action taken or threatened against the servicemember, or was a favorable personnel action withheld or threatened to be withheld following the protected communication?
3) Did the responsible management official have knowledge of the servicemember's protected communication or perceive the servicemember as making or preparing to make a protected communication?
4) Would the same personnel action have been taken, withheld, or threatened absent the protected communication?

Based on our review of randomly selected case files closed in fiscal year 2013, we estimate that the most common reason for closing a case was that DODIG determined that the responsible management official would have taken the personnel action absent the protected communication (question 4—37 percent), which means that the servicemember's protected communication did not have an effect on the responsible official's decision to take the personnel action. DODIG also closed cases because the servicemember did not make a protected communication (question 1—4 percent), there was no personnel action (question 2—9 percent), or the responsible management official who took the personnel action had no knowledge that the servicemember made or prepared to make a protected communication (question 3—3 percent). Additional reasons DODIG closed cases included timeliness—the servicemember did not file a reprisal complaint within 60 days of gaining knowledge of the personnel action—nonresponsive servicemembers, and withdrawals, among other reasons.[3] See figure 7 for DODIG's reasons for closing military reprisal cases by frequency.

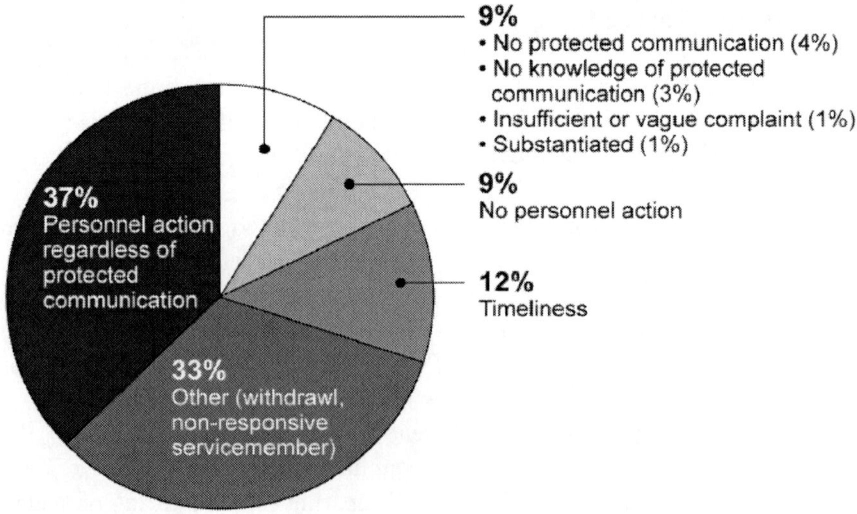

Source: GAO analysis of Department of Defense Inspector General (DODIG) data. | GAO-15-477.

Note: All percentage estimates in this figure have a margin of error of plus or minus 10 percentage points or fewer at the 95 percent confidence level.

Figure 7. Estimated Percentage of Reasons the Department of Defense (DOD) Closed Military Whistleblower Cases in Fiscal Year 2013.

Further, based on our case-file review of cases closed in fiscal year 2013, we estimate that the service IGs closed the majority of cases in fiscal year 2013 (70 percent) after conducting a preliminary inquiry and prior to a full investigation.

Substantiation Rates

Our analysis of DODIG data on military whistleblower reprisal cases closed in fiscal year 2014 shows that DODIG substantiated 9 percent of the cases that were fully investigated by DODIG investigators. In addition, our analysis shows that the service IGs substantiated 6 percent of cases that proceeded past the intake phase. DODIG officials stated that they calculate substantiation rates by the number of cases substantiated out of the number of cases fully investigated; however, as discussed in the report, we are unable to report on the total number of cases fully investigated by the service IGs because DODIG's data were not reliable for this purpose. As such, we report the service IGs' substantiation rates out of the number of cases that proceeded to further investigation after meeting the general intake requirements—a personnel action following a protected communication. See table 6 for fiscal year 2013 and 2014 substantiation rates.

Table 6. Department of Defense's (DOD) Substantiation Rates for Military Whistleblower Cases Closed in Fiscal Years 2013 and 2014

Investigating organization and case type	Number of cases substantiated, fiscal year2013	Percentage of cases substantiated, fiscal year 2013	Number of cases substantiated, fiscal year 2014	Percent of cases substantiated, fiscal year 2014
Department of Defense Inspector General (DODIG) full investigations	3	19%	2	9%
Service Inspector General (IG) preliminary inquiries and full investigations	18	6	21	6
All preliminary inquiries and full investigations	21	5	23	5
All cases closed by DODIG and the service IGs	21	4	23	4

Source: GAO analysis of Department of Defense Inspector General (DODIG) data. | GAO-15-477

End Notes

[1] The Office of Personnel Management administers the Federal Employee Viewpoint Survey annually to provide insight into the challenges agency leaders face in ensuring the federal government has an effective workforce. Office of Personnel Management, *2014 Federal Employee Viewpoint Survey Results, Department of Defense Agency Management Report.*

[2] Office of Personnel Management, *Department of Defense Office of Inspector General 2014 Employee Viewpoint Survey* (Aug. 4, 2014).

[3] GAO, *Whistleblower Protection: Actions Needed to Improve DOD's Military Whistleblower Reprisal Program*, GAO-12-362 (Washington, D.C.: Feb. 22, 2012). For a list of other GAO reports on whistleblower issues, see the Related GAO Products page at the end of this report.

[4] In the February 2012 report we made a total of eleven recommendations, including recommendations to address corrective action reporting and consistent monitoring of

reprisal investigations, among others. As of April 2015, DOD had implemented three of the eleven recommendations, and had actions underway to address the other eight.

[5] Department of Defense Directive 7050.06, *Military Whistleblower Protection* (Jul. 23, 2007) defines the military department IGs as including the IG of the Army, the Naval IG, the IG of the Air Force, and the Deputy Naval IG for Marine Corps Matters (Marine Corps IG). In this report, we refer to these organizations collectively as the service IGs. DOD reissued DOD Directive 7050.06 on April 17, 2015 to update its policy on military whistleblower protection and to incorporate recent changes to 10 U.S.C. § 1034. This report will hereinafter refer to DOD Directive 7050.06, dated July 23, 2007, unless otherwise stated because it was the applicable DOD guidance in effect to the military whistleblower case files we reviewed.

[6] We also collected data from DODIG for cases closed in fiscal year 2012; however, we did not use these data because DODIG transitioned to a new case management system in December 2012 and as a result of the data migration the fiscal year 2012 data are not reliable, according to DODIG officials.

[7] Project Management Institute, Inc. *A Guide to the Project Management Body of Knowledge (PMBOK® Guide)*, Fifth Edition, 2013.

[8] CIGIE is an independent entity established within the executive branch to address integrity, economy, and effectiveness issues that transcend individual government agencies and aid in the establishment of a professional, well-trained, and highly skilled workforce in the offices of inspectors general.

[9] We did not interview Marine Corps IG field investigators because the Marine Corps conducts all whistleblower reprisal investigations at the headquarters level.

[10] National Defense Authorization Act, Fiscal Year 1989, Pub. L. No. 100-456, §846 (1988) codified at 10 U.S.C. § 1034, as amended. 10 U.S.C. § 1034 prohibits individuals from restricting a member of the armed forces (hereafter referred to as a servicemember) from making a lawful communication to a Member of Congress or an IG. It further prohibits individuals from taking or threatening to take an unfavorable personnel action as a reprisal against a servicemember for making or preparing to make a lawful communication to a Member of Congress or an IG or from communicating to a Member of Congress, IG, a member of the DOD audit, inspection, investigation, or law enforcement organization; any person or organization in the chain of command; a court-martial proceeding, or any other person or organization designated pursuant to regulations or other established administrative procedures for such communications regarding what the servicemember reasonably believes to be evidence of any of the following: a violation of law or regulation, including a law or regulation prohibiting rape, sexual assault, or other sexual misconduct, sexual harassment or unlawful discrimination, gross mismanagement, a gross waste of funds, an abuse of authority, or a substantial and specific danger to public health or safety, or a threat by another servicemember or civilian employee that indicates a determination or intent to kill or cause serious bodily injury to servicemembers or civilians or damage to military, federal, or civilian property.

[11] DOD Directive 7050.06.

[12] An unlawful communication is one that includes disclosures of classified, Privacy Act-protected, and medical quality assurance information to an unauthorized recipient, or threats according to Department of Defense Inspector General Departmental Guidance, *Guide to Investigating Military Whistleblower Reprisal and Restriction Complaints* (Oct. 29, 2014).

[13] See Pub. L. No. 113-66, §1714(b) (2013).

[14] DOD Directive 7050.06.

[15] DODIG Departmental Guidance, *Guide to Investigating Military Whistleblower Reprisal and Restriction Complaints*.

[16] DOD IG Departmental Guidance, *Guide to Investigating Military Whistleblower Reprisal and Restriction Complaints*.

[17] The Boards for the Correction of Military Records (BCMR) are military department organizations with responsibility for reviewing and taking action on applications for the correction of military records at the request of a servicemember. A servicemember may also petition the appropriate BCMR as a result of any IG determination across DOD, such as when a reprisal complaint is not substantiated.

[18] GAO-12-362.

[19] Department of Defense Inspector General Memorandum, *Government Accountability Office (GAO) Report on Whistleblower Protection: Actions Needed to Improve DOD's Military Whistleblower Reprisal Program* (Feb. 24, 2012).

[20] This estimate has a margin of error of plus or minus 9 percentage points at the 95 percent confidence level.

[21] This estimate has a relative margin of error of plus or minus 20 percent of the estimate.

[22] This estimate has a relative margin of error of plus or minus 22 percent of the estimate.

[23] GAO, *Standards for Internal Control in the Federal Government*, GAO/AIMD-00-21.3.1 (Washington, D.C.: November 1999).

[24] GAO, *Whistleblower Protection: Additional Actions Needed to Improve DOJ's Handling of FBI Retaliation Complaints*, GAO-15-112 (Washington, D.C.: Jan. 23, 2015).

[25] This average does not include cases that DODIG dismissed after completing the intake process. In February 2012, we estimated that the average investigation time for all cases closed between January 1, 2009 and March 31, 2011 was 451 days, plus or minus 94 days based on a random sample. See GAO-12-362 for more information.

[26] We were not able, using DODIG's data, to distinguish between the number of cases that were fully investigated by the service IGs and the number that the services closed with some investigative work but prior to a full investigation. That number was not reliable for our purposes due to DODIG coding errors; however, those errors did not impact the overall number of reprisal cases.

[27] DODIG completes intake for complaints that servicemembers file with DODIG. The service IGs complete intake for complaints that servicemembers file with them. The service IGs do not consistently notify DODIG about complaints they receive and determine not to be reprisal allegations because those complaints do not meet DODIG's first two questions to determine the four elements of reprisal. Therefore, the service IGs do not track the length of the intake process for all these complaints.

[28] GAO-12-362.

[29] Deputy Secretary of Defense Memorandum, *Report on Task Force to Improve Timeliness of Senior Official Investigations* (Jan. 5, 2015).

[30] GAO-12-362.

[31] This estimate represents the lower bound of the 95 percent confidence interval around our estimate of the average difference between our calculation of total case time and DOD's timeliness metric.

[32] GAO-12-362.

[33] Council of the Inspectors General on Integrity and Efficiency, *Quality Standards for Investigations* (Nov. 15, 2011).

[34] This estimate has a margin of error of plus or minus 12 percentage points at the 95 percent confidence level. The service IGs do not consistently notify DODIG about complaints they

receive and determine not to be reprisal allegations because those complaints do not meet DODIG's first two questions to determine the four elements of reprisal. Therefore, neither DODIG nor the service IGs consistently track cases that servicemembers filed with the service IGs, but do not meet questions 1 and 2 of DODIG's questions to determine the four elements of reprisal.

[35] GAO/AIMD-00-21.3.1.

[36] Deputy Secretary of Defense Memorandum, *Report on Task Force to Improve Timeliness of Senior Official Investigations.*

[37] 10 U.S.C. § 2222 requires investment review and certification of certain defense business systems prior to obligation of funds to ensure that the business system complies with the enterprise architecture, among other conditions.

[38] *PMBOK* is a trademark of Project Management Institute, Inc.

[39] Project Management Institute, Inc. *A Guide to the Project Management Body of Knowledge (PMBOK® Guide)*, Fifth Edition, 2013.

[40] DOD Directive 7050.06.

[41] CIGIE, *Quality Standards for Investigations.*

[42] Council of the Inspectors General on Integrity and Efficiency, *Qualitative Assessment Review Guidelines for Investigative Operations of Federal Offices of Inspector General* (December 2011).

[43] DOD Inspector General Departmental Guidance, *Administrative Investigations Manual, Part I* (2012).

[44] This estimate has a margin of error of plus or minus 9 percentage points.

[45] 10 U.S.C. § 1034; DOD Directive 7050.06; DODIG Departmental Guidance, *Guide to Investigating Military Whistleblower Reprisal and Restriction Complaints.*

[46] CIGIE, *Quality Standards for Investigations.*

[47] GAO/AIMD-00-21.3.1.

[48] DODIG Departmental Guidance, *Guide to Investigating Military Whistleblower Reprisal and Restriction Complaints.*

[49] DOD can use discretion to investigate reprisal complaints that were submitted more than 1 year after the alleged personnel action took place based on compelling reasons for the delay in submission.

[50] DODIG Departmental Guidance, *Guide to Investigating Military Whistleblower Reprisal and Restriction Complaints.*

[51] DODIG Departmental Guidance, *Guide to Investigating Military Whistleblower Reprisal and Restriction Complaints.*

[52] This estimate represents the lower bound of the 95 percent confidence interval around our estimate of the percentage of service preliminary inquiries that were missing at least one element. Furthermore, we estimate that these cases were missing an average of two required elements.

[53] This estimate represents the lower bound of the 95 percent confidence interval around our estimate of the percentage of service full investigations that were missing at least one element. Furthermore, we estimate that these cases were missing an average of one required element.

[54] DODIG Departmental Guidance, *Guide to Investigating Military Whistleblower Reprisal and Restriction Complaints.* These estimates have a margin of error of plus or minus 11 and 17 percentage points respectively. Additionally, the difference between these two estimates is statistically significant at the 95 percent confidence level.

[55] CIGIE, *Quality Standards for Investigations.*

[56] DODIG Departmental Guidance, *Administrative Investigations Manual,* pt. I.
[57] DODIG Departmental Guidance, *Guide to Investigating Military Whistleblower Reprisal and Restriction Complaints.*
[58] GAO, *Government Auditing Standards*, GAO-12-331G (Washington, D.C.: Jan. 20, 2012).

End Note for Appendix I

[1] CIGIE is an independent entity established within the executive branch to address integrity, economy, and effectiveness issues that transcend individual government agencies and aid in the establishment of a professional, well-trained, and highly skilled workforce in the offices of inspectors general. Quality Standards for Investigations as defined by CIGIE include general standards relating to investigator independence and due professional care, such as the thoroughness, impartiality, objectivity, and timeliness of the investigation and whether the documentation is accurate and complete. CIGIE's qualitative standards relate to how the investigation is planned, executed, and reported as well as how the investigative information is managed.

End Notes for Appendix II

[1] Servicemembers making protected communications about sexual assault and sexual harassment were not always victims, and in some cases made the protected communications on behalf of another individual, including protected communications about how a sexual assault or harassment report was treated within the servicemember's command.
[2] A protected communication is any lawful communication to a Member of Congress or an IG or a communication made to certain appropriate officials that the individual reasonably believes to evidence violation of law or regulation, including a law or regulation prohibiting sexual assault or unlawful discrimination, gross mismanagement, a gross waste of funds or other resources, an abuse of authority, or a substantial and specific danger to public health or safety.
[3] Per the National Defense Authorization Act for fiscal year 2014, servicemembers have 1 year following the personnel action to file a reprisal complaint, an increase from 60 days, which was the requirement in place during fiscal year 2013, which is the scope of our file review.

In: Military Whistleblower Reprisal … ISBN: 978-1-63483-938-9
Editor: Jesse L. Porter

Chapter 2

GUIDE TO INVESTIGATING MILITARY WHISTLEBLOWER REPRISAL AND RESTRICTION COMPLAINTS[*]

Inspector General, Department of Defense

FOREWORD

This guide replaces the "Green Guide" (IGDG 7050.6, cancelled). It describes best practices for conducting military reprisal and restriction intakes and investigations. Please refer to DoDD 7050.06, "Military Whistleblower Protection," for policy and responsibilities for military whistleblower protection, to include notification requirements.

DISCLAIMER

This document is intended to provide guidance regarding some of the internal operations of the Department of Defense (DoD) and is solely for the benefit of the Government. No duties, rights, or benefits–substantive or procedural–are created or implied by this guide. The contents of this guide are not enforceable by any person or entity against DoD.

---

[*] This is an edited, reformatted and augmented version of document issued June 29, 2015.

SECTION 1. RESTRICTION AND WHISTLEBLOWER REPRISAL

1. Purpose

This Section explains restriction, reprisal, and the applicable legal and regulatory terms and their application, under Title 10, United States Code, Section 1034 (10 U.S.C. 1034), "Protected communications; prohibition of retaliatory actions," and DoD Directive (DoDD) 7050.06, "Military Whistleblower Protection," (Appendix A).

2. Restriction

Title 10 U.S.C. 1034 prohibits anyone from restricting a member of the Armed Forces from making lawful communications to a member of Congress or an Inspector General (IG).

Proving restriction requires establishing by a preponderance of the evidence that the responsible management official (RMO) prevented or attempted to prevent a member of the Armed Forces from making or preparing to make a lawful communication to a member of Congress or an IG. While as a general matter an RMO may not limit a member's communications to a member of Congress or an IG, in analyzing a case consider authorized limits on official communications such as those provided in DoDI 5400.04, "Provisions of Information to Congress"; DoD 5400.7-R, "DoD FOIA Program"; DoD 5400.11-R, "DoD Privacy Program." The determination is always case-specific and must take into consideration the totality of the circumstances in that case.

Restriction can be substantiated even if the RMO's attempt at preventing a lawful communication failed to actually deter the member of the Armed Forces from subsequently making contact with a member of Congress or an IG. When analyzing such a fact-pattern, your focus should be on whether a reasonable person could believe the RMO's action was an attempt to deter the member from talking to a member of Congress or an IG.

3. Whistleblower Reprisal

The elements of reprisal are protected communication (PC); knowledge of the protected communication on the part of the responsible management official; a personnel action (PA) taken, threatened, or withheld; and a causal connection between the PC and the PA. If the evidence establishes that the PA would have been taken, threatened, or withheld even absent the PC, then the complaint is not substantiated. All four elements of reprisal must be established by a preponderance of the evidence in order for reprisal to be substantiated. Each element is discussed in detail below.

a. Element 1, Protected Communication (PC): Did Complainant Make or Prepare to Make a Protected Communication, or Was Complainant Perceived As Having Made or Prepared to Make a Protected Communication?

The statute protects members of the Armed Forces who make or prepare to make a PC. Examples of preparing to make a PC include drafting but not sending a complaint and expressing an intention to make a PC. The statute also protects a member who is perceived as making or preparing to make a PC not actually made. The complainant may have written a letter, sent an email, or spoken to someone who can receive a PC. Determining whether the complainant's communication or perceived communication was protected, therefore, relies on two basic questions:

- What was communicated?
- To whom was it communicated?

Table 1.1 lists the content requirements and conditions under which communications are protected.

Members of Congress and IGs

"Any lawful communication to a Member of Congress or an IG" is protected under 10 U.S.C. 1034. Communications to Congress and IGs need not disclose wrongdoing to be protected; the only requirement is that the communication be lawful. Examples include routine constituent correspondence, complaints about chain of command, or testifying before Congress. Unlawful communications include disclosures of classified, Privacy Act-protected, and medical quality assurance information to an unauthorized recipient, or threats.

Table 1.1. Protected Communications

Type of Communication:	Conditions on Protection:	When made to:
Any communication	Must be a lawful communication	• A member of Congress or • An IG
Any communication in which a Service member communicates information that he or she reasonably believes evidences: • A violation of law or regulation, including a law or regulation prohibiting rape, sexual assault, or other sexual misconduct in violations of section 920 through 920c of Reference (c) (articles 120 through 120c of the UCMJ), sexual harassment or unlawful discrimination; • Gross mismanagement, a gross waste of funds or other resources, an abuse of authority, or a substantial and specific danger to public health or safety; or • A threat by another Service member or employee of the Federal Government that indicates a determination or intent to kill or cause serious bodily injury to Service members or civilians or damage to military, federal, or civilian property. • Testimony, or otherwise participating in or assisting in an investigation or proceeding related to a communication as described above; or • Filing, or causing to be filed, participating in, or otherwise assisting in a military whistleblower reprisal action.	A communication will not lose its protected status because: • The communication was made to a person who participated in the activity that the Service member complained of; • The communication revealed information that had been previously disclosed; • Of the Service member's motive for making the communication; • The communication was not in writing; • The communication was made while the Service member was off duty; or • The communication was made during the normal course of the Service member's duties.	• A member of Congress; • An IG; • A member of a DoD audit, inspection, investigation, or law enforcement organization; • Any person or organization in the chain of command; • A court-martial proceeding; or • Any other person or organization designated pursuant to regulations or other established administrative procedures to receive such communications

Officials authorized to receive PCs include:

- a member of Congress;
- an Inspector General;
- a member of a DoD audit, inspection, investigation, or law enforcement organization;
- any person or organization in the complainant's chain of command;
- a court martial proceeding; or
- any other person designated pursuant to regulations or other established administrative procedures to receive such communications.

Many organizations have been designated to receive communication related to their specific areas of responsibility. For example, safety officials are authorized to receive communications concerning violations of safety laws or regulations, the Sexual Assault Response Coordinator is authorized to receive communications concerning sexual violence, and Equal Opportunity advisors are authorized to receive communications regarding equal opportunity, discrimination, or harassment issues.

Communication made to an authorized recipient listed above is a PC only if the member communicates (or is perceived as communicating) information reasonably believed to constitute evidence of:

- a violation of law or regulation to include a law or regulation prohibiting rape, sexual assault, or other sexual misconduct in violation of articles 120 through 120c of the Uniform Code of Military Justice, sexual harassment, or unlawful discrimination;
- gross mismanagement, a gross waste of funds, an abuse of authority, or a substantial and specific danger to public health or safety; or
- a threat by another member of the Armed Forces or employee of the Federal Government that indicates a determination or intent to kill or cause serious bodily injury to members of the Armed Forces or civilians, or damage to military, Federal, or civilian property.

A belief is reasonable if a disinterested observer with knowledge of the essential facts known to and readily ascertainable by the complainant could reasonably conclude that the disclosed information evidences one of the categories of wrongdoing. So long as his or her belief is reasonable, the complainant need not be right about the underlying allegation.

b. Element 2, Personnel Action (PA): Was an Unfavorable Personnel Action Taken or Threatened Against Complainant, or Was a Favorable Personnel Action Withheld or Threatened to Be Withheld from Complainant?

The statute prohibits persons from taking or threatening to take unfavorable PAs or withholding or threatening to withhold favorable PAs in reprisal for PC. DoDD 7050.06 defines a personnel action as "any action taken on a member of the Armed Forces that affects, or has the potential to affect, that military member's current position or career." PAs include promotion, a disciplinary or corrective action; a transfer or reassignment; a performance evaluation; a decision on pay, benefits, awards, or training; referral for a mental health evaluation; or any other significant change in duties or responsibilities inconsistent with the military member's grade.

Unfavorable Personnel Actions

Unfavorable PAs may be administrative action that takes away a benefit or results in an entry or document added to the affected person's personnel records that could be considered negative by boards or supervisors. Each Service has regulations governing PAs.

Examples of actions generally considered unfavorable PAs include:

- counseling that is punitive or that supports separation or adverse evaluation
- letter of reprimand, caution, censure
- adverse evaluation report
- relief for cause
- removal from position
- relief of command
- return to service
- separation from service
- removal from promotion, school, or command list
- entry-level separation
- administrative reduction in rank or pay
- bar to reenlistment
- military occupational specialty reclassification
- referral for mental health evaluation

Examples of favorable PAs that can be withheld or threatened to be withheld include:

- evaluation
- promotion recommendation
- award
- training
- assignment
- attendance at school
- transfer

Examples of threatened PAs taken from actual cases where a reasonable person might infer a threat include:

- a subordinate's career would be "crushed and destroyed" for filing an IG complaint;
- the statement that a complainant would suffer a "new set of headaches" come evaluation time if he or she filed an IG complaint; and
- an RMO telling a complainant that talking to the IG was "not career enhancing."

The list of PAs above is not exhaustive. The directive's broad definition of PA requires investigators to consider each alleged PA on a case-by-case basis to determine whether the action had or may have an effect on the complainant's current position or career.

Investigators should review, on a case-by-case basis, complaints that involve counseling to determine whether they affect, or have the potential to affect, a Service member's current position or career. The same applies for other locally held letters of reprimand, admonishment, instruction, or censure.

In evaluating these complaints, the facts regarding the nature of the action should be adequately developed before deciding on whether to dismiss the complaint or proceed to investigation.

Favorable Personnel Actions

Withholding a favorable PA can affect a member's current position or career as adversely as taking unfavorable action.

An RMO's recommendation for a choice assignment may or may not be a PA. Careers are built on a series of assignments with follow-on assignments building on previous ones. Some programs, schools, and assignments weigh command recommendations, but others do not. Examine what influence the recommendation would have on the decision maker.

Most favorable PAs are included in the member's Official Military Personnel Folder (OMPF). Evaluations, assignments, school attendance, and awards are generally considered PAs because of their long-lasting impact on a career. Promotion and other career boards review and consider the schools attended and awards received. However, not all schools have an impact.

Additional duties are not generally considered PAs. They do not change the inherent nature of a Service member's current position and normally will not impact the complainant's career. The OMPF usually does not record a Service member's additional duties. Certain additional duties may be desirable; however, it is unlikely even in those circumstances that the additional duty would be considered a PA.

Determining whether an action is a PA may require additional fact finding. If you are uncertain of whether the action had the potential to impact the complainant's current position or career, consult with a subject matter expert, such as contacting Human Resources Command for an expert opinion concerning an OER or NCOER to discuss what, if any, impact the RMO's actions could have on the complainant's current position or career.

c. Element 3, Knowledge: Did the Responsible Management Official(s) Have Knowledge of Complainant's Protected Communication(s) or Perceive Complainant As Making or Preparing Protected Communication(s)?

Independently analyze each RMO involved in the PA(s) to determine his or her knowledge of the PC. The RMO may assert that he or she was unaware of the PC. If the RMO did not know about the PC, then he or she could not have taken or threatened a PA in reprisal for a PC. However, it is very difficult to prove an absence of knowledge. Compare the RMO's testimony with other evidence, including the testimony of complainant and other witnesses, and assign it appropriate weight and credibility.

Sometimes RMOs take action based on rumor or perception. The rumors or perceptions may not be accurate, but they can still motivate reprisal.

d. Element 4, Causation: Would the Same Personnel Action(s) Have Been Taken, Withheld, or threatened Absent the Protected Communication(s)?

To determine the answer to the "causation" question, we must analyze what bearing, if any, the protected communication had on the decision to take, threaten, or withhold the personnel action. For each personnel action, we analyze the following factors and then weigh them together to determine whether the PA would have been taken absent the PC.

Reason Stated by RMO for Taking, Withholding, or Threatening the PA

Examine the evidence supporting the RMO's stated reason for the PA. If the reason was performance related, what documentation exists regarding performance in support of the PA? Is there supporting testimonial evidence? If the RMO stated that he or she took an action based on the complainant's poor duty performance but a preponderance of evidence indicated that the complainant was a good performer, the RMO's stated reason has not been proven.

Timing between the Protected Communication(s) and Personnel Action(s)

The importance of producing an accurate chronology cannot be overstated. A PA taken shortly after the complainant's PC supports the inference of reprisal. To the contrary, the RMO may have taken the PA months or even years after the complainant's PC. The complainant may have been in a different assignment or command when he or she made the PC. Consider whether the same management officials affected by the underlying investigation or PC were still in a position to take or influence the PA.

The RMO may provide evidence that he or she made the decision prior to the PC. The RMO may also provide evidence that he or she contemplated or discussed taking the action with other individuals prior to the PC. If the RMO consulted with others prior to taking the action, those individuals can provide relevant evidence and should be interviewed to determine whether they corroborate or refute the stated reason for taking the action.

Motive on the Part of the RMO(s) to Reprise

Did the RMO suffer embarrassment or negative consequences arising from the PC? In addition, have any of the RMOs exhibited or expressed animosity toward the complainant for making the PC, or have they expressed animosity regarding the very idea of, for example, filing an IG complaint or contacting a member of Congress? For instance, you may find evidence that the RMO displayed anger in response to learning of the complainant's PC because he or she believed it had a negative impact on their career, or it was embarrassing to the command. Even when an RMO offers an "independent basis" for a PA (that is, asserts that the PC was not a factor and something else was the only factor), the investigation is not complete until the investigator tests the assertion against the evidence and considers the totality of the circumstances surrounding the PA.

Disparate Treatment of Complainant As Compared to Other Similarly Situated Individuals Who Did Not Make PCS

If similarly situated personnel who did not make a PC exist, consider whether the RMO's actions were consistent with actions he or she has taken against those personnel. A similarly situated person would be one who engaged in the same conduct or whose performance was at a similar level to the complainant's. If the RMO treated the complainant the same as other similarly situated military members who had not made PCs, then the evidence supports that the RMO did not reprise. If the RMO disciplined the complainant more severely than others who had not made a PC, then the evidence supports reprisal. If the complainant's performance was the stated reason for the PA, how did the RMO treat other poor performers? Were they given more chances to improve before receiving a comparable PA or was poor performance generally overlooked?

4. Standard of Proof

The standard of proof in 10 U.S.C. 1034 cases is a preponderance of the evidence, meaning that degree of relevant evidence that a reasonable person, considering the record as a whole, would accept as sufficient to find that a contested fact is more likely to be true than untrue.

SECTION 2. COMPLAINT INTAKE

1. Expeditious Determination of Whether Sufficient Evidence Exists to Warrant Investigation

Title 10, United States Code, Section 1034, and DoD Directive 7050.06 require that Inspectors General who receive a military reprisal allegation must "expeditiously determine ... whether there is sufficient evidence to warrant an investigation of the allegation." Investigators should use the intake form at Appendix B when conducting intakes.

2. Prima Facie Determination

The DoD OIG has implemented a streamlined complaint intake process for investigators to determine whether complaints alleging reprisal provide sufficient evidence to warrant an investigation. For purposes of deciding whether to investigate, view the complainant's assertions in the light most favorable to the complainant and analyze the following factors:

a) **Timeliness?** Did the complainant file the complaint within one year of the date on which the complainant became aware of the personnel action?
b) **Protected Communication?** Has the complainant alleged that he or she made or was preparing to make a protected communication, or was he or she perceived as having made a protected communication?
c) **Personnel Action?** Has the complainant alleged that an unfavorable personnel action was taken or threatened against him or her, or was a favorable personnel action withheld or threatened to be withheld from him or her?
d) **Knowledge?** Does the complaint, as supplemented by an interview of the complainant, support an inference that the RMO had knowledge of the PC or perceive the complainant as making or preparing to make a PC?
e) **Causation?** Does the complaint, as supplemented by an interview of the complainant, support an inference of reprisal? That is, do the facts as set forth in the complaint and clarified in an interview of the complainant suggest a causal connection between the PC and the PA? This threshold can be met where the facts suggest the existence of one or more of the following:
    - The PA followed closely behind the PC
    - The PC was about something that would give the RMO motive to reprise or the RMO has expressed animosity toward the PC
    - The complainant received worse treatment than others who had not made PCs

The matrix in Figure 2.1 is a reference tool to help determine whether a communication is protected or a personnel action is covered under 10 U.S.C. 1034.

<table>
<tr><td rowspan="4">10 U.S.C. 1034 "PROTECTED COMMUNICATION; PROHIBITION OF RETALIATORY PERSONNEL ACTIONS"

DoD Directive 7050.06, "Military Whistleblower Protection"</td><td colspan="3">(a) PROHIBITION OF RESTRICTION</td></tr>
<tr><td colspan="3">No person may restrict a member of the armed forces in lawfully communicating with a Member of Congress or an IG.</td></tr>
<tr><td colspan="3">(b) PROHIBITION OF RETALIATORY PERSONNEL ACTIONS</td></tr>
<tr><td>PROTECTED COMMUNICATION</td><td>TO</td><td>PERSONNEL ACTIONS</td></tr>
<tr><td></td><td>(b)(1) Making or preparing or being perceived as making or preparing:
(A) Any lawful communication to a Member of Congress or an Inspector General (IG)

(B) Information reasonably believed to evidence:
• A violation of law or regulation, including a law or regulation prohibiting rape, sexual assault, or other sexual misconduct in violation of articles 120 through 120c of the UCMJ, sexual harassment or unlawful discrimination.
• Gross mismanagement, a gross waste of funds, an abuse of authority, or a substantial and specific danger to public health or safety.
• A threat that indicates a member's or federal employee's determination or intent to kill or cause serious bodily injury to members or civilians or damage to military, federal or civilian property

(C)
• Testifying or participating in or assisting in an investigation or proceeding related to a PC
• Filing, causing to be filed, participating in, or otherwise assisting in an action under this section</td><td>(b)(1)

(A) Member of Congress or Inspector General

(B)
• Member of Congress
• Inspector General
• Member of a Department of Defense audit, inspection, investigation, or law enforcement organization
• Any person or organization in the chain of command
• A court-martial proceeding
• Any other person or organization designated pursuant to regulations or other established administrative procedures for such communications.</td><td>• Taking an unfavorable personnel action
• Threatening to take an unfavorable personnel action
• Withholding a favorable personnel action
• Threatening to withhold a favorable personnel action
• Making or threatening to make a significant change in the duties or responsibilities of a member of the armed forces not commensurate with the member's grade

DoDD 7050.06: Any action that affects, or has the potential to affect, the military member's current position or career, including:
• promotion
• disciplinary/corrective action
• transfer or reassignment
• performance evaluation
• decisions concerning pay, benefits, awards, or training
• relief or removal
• separation or discharge
• referral for mental health eval
• any other significant change in duties/responsibilities inconsistent with the member's grade</td></tr>
</table>

Figure 2.1. Determining covered PC or PA.

3. Intake Process

The intake process includes five steps: (1) review the entire complaint, (2) initial contact with the complainant, (3) an intake interview of the complainant, (4) clarification of the allegation with the complainant, and (5) a recommendation to dismiss[1] the case without full investigation or proceed to investigation.

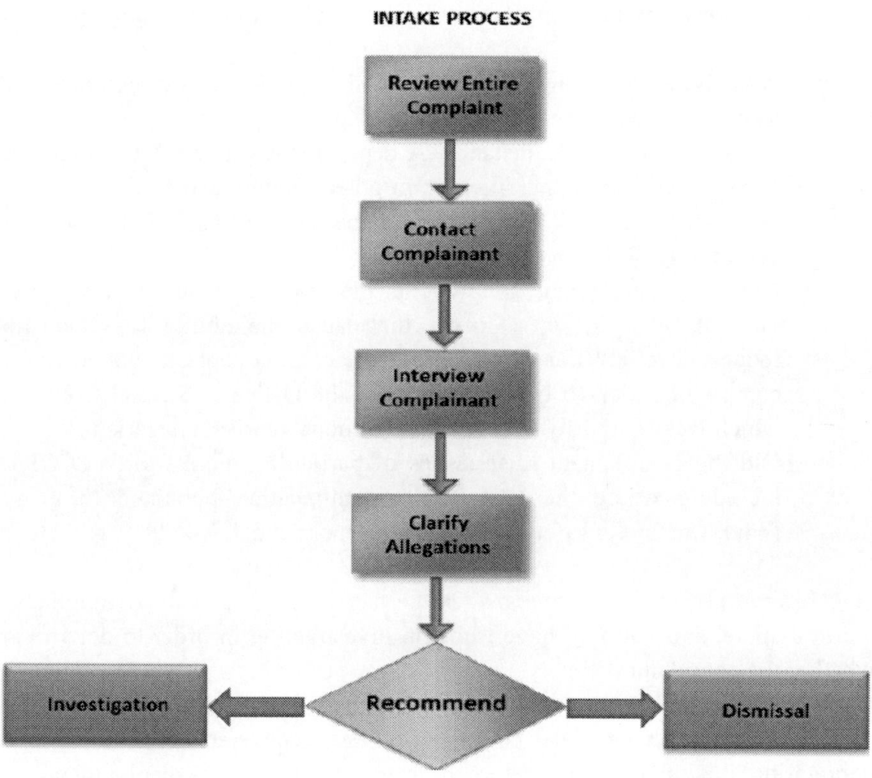

Figure 2.2. Intake Process.

a. Review the Entire Complaint and Its Timeline

Begin by reading the entire reprisal complaint and determine whether it is timely. No investigation is required when a member or former member of the Armed Forces submits a complaint of reprisal more than 1 year after the date

1 'We use "dismiss" to mean closing a case following intake, for failure to make a prima facie allegation, or for other threshold reasons such as timeliness.

that the member became aware of the personnel action that is the subject of the allegation. The year begins when the RMO's decision to take the PA has been made and communicated to the complainant; the complainant has 1 year from that time to file his or her complaint. A complaint of reprisal submitted more than 1 year after the decision was made and communicated to the complainant may, nevertheless, be considered based on compelling reasons for the delay in submission or the strength of the evidence submitted. Before making a recommendation to dismiss or investigate the case, carefully examine the reason or reasons why the complainant did not file his or her allegation timely:

- Was there something extraordinary that prevented the complainant from filing the complaint earlier? A deployment in and of itself is not an extraordinary circumstance. A deployment where the complainant had no access to phone, internet, or other communication devices may be extraordinary. Illness would not be extraordinary, but a serious debilitating illness or injury might be.
- Did the complainant timely file the precise claim at issue but mistakenly do so in a forum that lacks the ability to grant the requested relief? For example, did the complainant attempt to file a complaint under 10 U.S.C. 1034 with the Office of Special Counsel, which lacks authority to investigate military reprisal allegations?
- Did the complainant raise issues of particular interest to DoD OIG, including where the protected communication pertained to gross fraud, warfighter safety, detainee abuse, or sexual assault?

However, there will be times when the facts needed to evaluate timeliness are in dispute, and you will have to begin investigating in order to determine whether the complaint is timely.

Even if circumstances support extending the filing deadline, the extension is not indefinite. Once the complainant has recovered from a serious debilitating illness or injury, returned from an inaccessible deployment, or been informed of the correct forum, the complainant must promptly file the complaint or risk untimely filing.

b. Contact the Complainant

After familiarizing yourself with the entire complaint, contact the complainant promptly to conduct or schedule the intake interview.

If you are unable to interview the complainant upon contact, schedule an interview as soon as is practicable. Your first contact should accomplish at least the following:

- Inform the complainant that you have received his/her complaint and need to interview him or her to determine whether sufficient evidence exists to warrant an investigation.
- Ask the complainant to mail, email, or bring to the interview copies of any written protected communications and documents related to personnel actions.
- Briefly explain the investigative process and, if necessary, briefly explain whistleblower reprisal.
- Ensure that the complainant understands that if you proceed to full investigation, you will be asking for the names and contact information for witnesses who can testify as to what happened and that he or she may provide additional relevant evidence at any time.

c. Interview the Complainant and Clarify the Allegations

The purpose of the intake interview with the complainant is to ensure that the investigator has obtained a thorough understanding of what the complainant has alleged and clarified any questions that need to be resolved before making a prima facie determination. During an intake interview, investigators should ordinarily discuss with the complainant every PC alleged to be a factor in the alleged PA(s), in chronological order. Additionally, the investigator should obtain as much detail as possible regarding PAs, including the names of individuals involved and the names of the organizations involved. Dates are particularly important to determine the timeliness of the allegations as well as to evaluate whether an inference of reprisal is apparent. Ask the complainant to send you any available documentation pertaining to the protected communication(s) and the personnel action(s).

The investigator should focus the interview on the PCs, PAs, and any information that suggests the possible existence of a causal connection between the PCs and the PAs. To explore the causal connection, ask questions pertaining to why the complainant believes the actions were taken in reprisal.

Ordinarily, questioning will proceed chronologically through the fact pattern. Organizing the topics of questioning around the elements of reprisal may assist in focusing the interview. Below are some sample questions that will need to be asked in almost every intake:

PCs

- To whom did you make your protected communications?
- What did you communicate to them?
- When did you make each protected communication?

Pas

- What personnel action was taken, withheld, threatened?
- Who was the RMO that took the action or made the threat?
- Were there other individuals involved in recommending, approving, or influencing the personnel action?
- What was each official's role in each action?
- Do you believe that the official(s) knew about the PC? Why?

Causation

- Why do you believe the action taken, withheld, or threatened was in reprisal?
- What motive would the RMO have to reprise against you?
- What were the reasons provided to you by the RMO for the action they took, threatened, or withheld?
- Did you do what they said you did?

Before ending the intake interview, summarize and recap what you believe the complainant has said. As soon as possible following the intake interview, investigators must memorialize the interview in writing.

d. Underlying Allegation

Title 10 U.S.C. 1034 and DoD Directive 7050.06 require that the Inspector General receiving the allegation of reprisal conduct a separate investigation of the alleged wrongdoing that was the substance of the protected communication.

It is important during the intake process for investigators to obtain information from the complainant to ensure that the complainant's original alleged wrongdoing has been investigated or addressed in the proper channels. These matters should be referred to the appropriate authority for review.

4. Allegations of Restriction

Allegations of restriction are not subject to the 1 year filing deadline. They are also unique in that they are not analyzed according to the elements of reprisal.

Rather, the single question at issue is whether a preponderance of the evidence established that the RMO restricted or attempted to restrict a military member from making a lawful communication to a member of Congress or an IG. Accordingly, interview questions should focus on what was done or said to restrict the member.

5. Recommend Dismissal or Proceed to Investigation

If the investigator determines that either no PC or PA occurred, the investigator should stop and draft a proposed dismissal of the complaint. The proposed dismissal must be provided to the DoD OIG for approval.

In order to be timely and efficient, the investigator should limit the intake process to a prima facie determination and not conduct a lengthy preliminary inquiry to determine if the allegations are substantiated or not. Properly executing the intake process is critical to supporting a dismissal or laying the foundation for a successful investigation.

SECTION 3. INVESTIGATIONS

1. Introduction

The Council of the Inspectors General on Integrity and Efficiency (CIGIE) "Quality Standards for Investigations," dated November 2011, establishes the professional standards and principles for investigators of the Federal Offices of Inspectors General. CIGIE standards require that investigators conduct investigations in a timely, efficient, thorough, and objective manner.

a. Independence

Under the CIGIE general standards for "independence," the investigative organization must be free, both in fact and appearance, from impairments to independence.

Accordingly, under 10 U.S.C. 1034, the Inspector General conducting the investigation must be outside the immediate chain of command of both the member submitting the allegation and the individual or individuals alleged to have taken the retaliatory action.

b. Due Professional Care

The CIGIE Standards require that "due professional care" be used in conducting investigations. Due professional care requires:

> **Thoroughness.** All investigations must be conducted in a diligent and complete manner, and reasonable steps should be taken to ensure pertinent issues are sufficiently resolved.
>
> **Objectivity.** Evidence must be gathered and reported in an unbiased and independent manner in an effort to determine the validity of an allegation or to resolve an issue.
>
> **Timeliness.** All investigations must be conducted and reported with due diligence and in a timely manner. This is especially critical given the impact investigations have on the lives of individuals and activities of organizations.
>
> **Documentation.** The investigative report's findings must be supported by adequate documentation.
>
> **Legal.** Investigations should be conducted in accordance with all applicable laws, rules and regulations, and with due respect for the rights and privacy of those involved.

This Section guides the investigator in conducting a reprisal investigation in a manner consistent with the CIGIE professional standards.

2. Planning the Investigation

Investigators should develop an investigative plan at the initiation of the investigation (see Appendix C for the investigative plan template). The first CIGIE Qualitative Standard is planning, which provides that "case-specific priorities must be established and objectives developed to ensure that individual case tasks are performed efficiently and effectively."

In reprisal investigations, the investigative plan should be focused on the elements of reprisal.

a. Element 1, Protected Communication (PC): Did Complainant Make or Prepare to Make a Protected Communication, or Was Complainant Perceived As Having Made or Prepared to Make a Protected Communication?

Identify each PC with specific information including the date the PC was made, the individual or organization that received the PC, and the specifics of the PC.

b. Element 2, Personnel Action (PA): Was an Unfavorable Personnel Action Taken or Threatened Against Complainant, or Was a Favorable Personnel Action Withheld or Threatened to Be Withheld from Complainant?

Identify each PA alleged to be reprisal by the complainant including the date of the PA and the Responsible Management Official (RMO) who took, threatened, or withheld the PA.

c. Element 3, Knowledge: Did the Responsible Management Official(s) Have Knowledge of Complainant's Protected Communication(s) or Perceive Complainant As Making or Preparing Protected Communication(s)?

Identify all RMOs including their rank, title, and organization. Identify whether those who were involved in the PA(s) were likely to have known about the PCs or have perceived Complainant to have made the PCs.

d. Element 4, Causation: Would the Same Personnel Action(s) Have Been Taken, Withheld, or Threatened Absent the Protected Communication(s)?

Plan the investigation to determine the following information in order to reach a conclusion whether reprisal occurred:

> Reason stated by each RMO for taking, withholding, or threatening action. Timing between the PC(s) and PA(s) – Was the PA taken after the PC?
>
> Motive on the part of the RMO(s) for deciding, taking, or withholding the PA. What bearing, if any, did the PC have on the decision to take or withhold the PA? Did the Complainant's PC allege any wrongdoing by any of the RMOs or otherwise implicate or criticize their performance, integrity, competence, or leadership? In addition, have any of the RMOs exhibited or expressed animosity toward the complainant for making the PC, or have they expressed animosity

regarding the very idea of, for example, filing an IG complaint or contacting a member of Congress?

Disparate treatment of Complainant as compared to other similarly situated individuals who did not make PCs: how did the RMO(s) respond in the past to similarly situated personnel who did not make PCs? Are their actions in the case of the Complainant consistent with past actions, or did they handle the matter differently? If the RMO(s) deviated from the way they normally acted in the past, you must explain the difference and determine whether the reasons are credible under the circumstances.

The investigator should assess what evidence is needed in order to resolve each element of reprisal.

- witnesses to be interviewed;
- documentary and other relevant evidence to be collected;
- investigation milestones; and
- steps necessary to execute a timely, efficient, thorough, and objective investigation

e. Develop a List of Documents

During the planning phase of your investigation identify documentary evidence that you believe will help resolve the allegation(s). Organize the documents needed by each PC and PA.

Examples of documents in reprisal investigations include copies of the PC to an IG, member of Congress, or Equal Opportunity office; copies of the PA, which may be found in official personnel files, as well as performance evaluations, counselings, awards; copies of disciplinary actions including letters of reprimand; and copies of separation, re-enlistment, and reduction actions. Emails, memorandums, other correspondence, and staffing packages are also often useful as evidence.

f. Develop a Witness List

The Investigative Plan should include a list of witnesses to be interviewed. It may be helpful to use an investigative planning tool like the Evidence Matrix at figure 3.1 below to accomplish this task. A list of witnesses can be developed based on the intake interview with the complainant, a review of documents obtained at the intake stage, and by performing research about the people and organizations involved in the investigation. Whenever possible, review documents that show the organizational structure and the chain of command.

The investigative plan should also address: Whom are you going to interview? In what sequence are you going to conduct the interviews? How many witnesses will need to be interviewed to ascertain the facts in the case? In order to conduct an objective investigation, investigators should interview the complainant, the RMOs, and relevant witnesses.

g. Develop a Chronology

Investigators will develop a chronology during the planning process. The chronology should contain details on who, what, when, where, how, and why things happened the way they did. The chronology will be updated and maintained throughout the investigation and will be critical in performing the timing analysis required to reach conclusions on whether reprisal occurred.

h. Planning Tools

There are planning tools that can help you organize your investigation. Lists of the documents to be obtained and witnesses to be interviewed are a good place to start. The evidence matrix below in Figure 3.1 is another tool that can help plan and organize the evidence. List the elements of reprisal along the horizontal axis. The vertical axis contains a list of witnesses, documents, and RMOs. Initially, where you expect a witness, document, or RMO to provide evidence will be marked with an "X." After you gather evidence, then the investigator can replace the "X" with the relevant credible evidence gathered. Additionally, you can place a "-" if you believe they may be knowledgeable about the allegation. A marking, "~" means do not discuss this part of the allegation with this witness.

Evidence Matrix				
Witness or Document	PC	PA	Knowledge	Causation
CDR Teller (Complainant)	X	X	-	
Col Abel (Chief of Staff)	X	~	-	
RADM Thomas (Commander)	X	~	-	
Mr. Dawn (Co-worker)	~	~	-	
Performance Evaluation	~	~	-	
Col Kenny (Subject)	X	X	X	X
Ms. Fawn (Subject)	X	X	X	X
X = Primary Witness	- = Discuss if knowledgeable ~ = Do not discuss			

Figure 3.1. Evidence Matrix.

3. The Investigation Process

The following steps of the investigative process are mandatory for all investigations.

a. Interview the Complainant

The complainant must always be interviewed. Frequently, follow-up interviews may be needed to go over new evidence or information developed during the investigation, and to clarify conflicts in testimony or ambiguities.

b. Obtain Relevant Documentation

Make sure to obtain relevant documentation whenever such documentation exists and is available to you.

c. Interview Knowledgeable Witnesses

Witnesses with knowledge of the events under investigation should be interviewed. It is important to interview relevant witnesses identified by the complainant and those identified by the RMO in order to be objective.

d. Interview the RMO

It is important to interview the RMO. This affords the RMO the opportunity to respond to the allegations made against them, to identify witnesses and evidence that may be material to the elements of reprisal. However, if initial fieldwork reveals that there was, in fact, no PC, interviewing the RMO will not be necessary.

e. Obtain a Legal Review

All final reports of investigation must undergo a legal review by an attorney with the servicing Staff Judge Advocate or General Counsel.

4. Interrogatories

Preparation is the key to timely, efficient, thorough, and objective interviews. Prepare an interrogatory before every interview. A well thought-out interrogatory is critical to a successful interview because it can help keep you properly focus on the issues under investigation. Referring to your well-developed interrogatory can also help you get back on track with your interview when unexpected issues or allegations arise. Always prepare your interrogatory before the interview, give thought to the order of your questions, and prepare open-ended questions whenever possible.

Building an interrogatory begins with the elements of reprisal and your assessment of the evidence you believe the witness possesses. The interrogatory provides a road map for the interview and helps ensure that the interview is thorough, accurate, and complete. If you plan to have the witness comment on documentary evidence, ensure that you have the documents ready and organized for introduction during the course of the interview. Build topics of questioning around the elements of reprisal, anticipate possible answers the witness might provide, and be prepared to ask appropriate follow-up questions. Interviewers who adequately prepare are rarely surprised and usually get better information from interviews.

In general, the questions below will form the foundation of your interrogatories, adapted to the type of witness being interviewed.

Element 1, Protected Communication (PC): Did Complainant Make or Prepare to Make a Protected Communication, or Was Complainant Perceived As Having Made or Prepared to Make a Protected Communication?

  - What was the PC? Describe the details of the communication. Provide a copy.
  - Who was the PC made to?
  - When was the PC made? Give the specific dates.
- If complainant prepared a PC or expressed intent to make a PC, ask:
  - Who knew about your preparation of the PC, or who knew you intended to make the PC?
  - How did they know?
  - Were there other witnesses?

Element 2, Personnel Action (PA): Was an Unfavorable Personnel Action Taken or Threatened Against Complainant, or Was a Favorable Personnel Action Withheld or Threatened to Be Withheld from Complainant?

- What personnel action(s) were taken or were withheld or were threatened?
- Who was the RMO who took, withheld, or threatened the action?
- Did other officials or members of the chain of command recommend or approve the action?
- On what date(s) did the action occur?

- Why would the action taken affect Complainant's position or career?
- Provide copies of all documents and related correspondence and emails.

Element 3, Knowledge: Did the Responsible Management Official(s) Have Knowledge of Complainant's Protected Communication(s) or Perceive Complainant As Making or Preparing Protected Communication(s)?

- Ask complainant:
  - Why do you believe that RMO knew about the PC?
  - Who did you tell about making or preparing a PC?
  - Who can testify that RMO knew about the PC?
  - Do you have any documents that show RMO knew about the PC?
- Ask witnesses:
  - Did you know that Complainant made a PC?
  - How did you find out?
  - When did you find out?
  - Did you tell anyone else?
  - Who else may know that the Complainant made a PC?
  - Do you have information that shows that the RMO knew that the Complainant made a PC?
  - Do you have any documents that show the Complainant made a PC?
- Ask the RMO:
  - Were you aware that the Complainant made or prepared a PC?
  - When did you become aware?
  - How did you become aware?
  - Did you suspect that the Complainant made a PC?
  - Did you hear rumors that the Complainant made a PC?

Element 4, Causation: Would the Same Personnel Action(s) Have Been Taken, Withheld, or Threatened Absent the Protected Communication(s)?

- Ask the complainant:
  - What reasons did the RMO give you for taking or withholding the PA?
  - Did you do those things?
  - Why do you believe the PA was taken in reprisal and not for the reasons given?

- Did anyone tell you they believed the PA was reprisal?
- Who else can corroborate the information that you have provided?
- Do you believe that you were treated differently than others were treated in similar situations?
- What examples can you give?
- Do you have any documents that relate to the PA?

- Ask witnesses:
  - Have you ever talked to the RMO about the PA being taken against the Complainant? When?
  - If so, what did the RMO say regarding the reasons for taking the PA?
  - Did the RMO mention the Complainant's PC? When? To whom?
  - Did you ever discuss the Complainant's PC with the RMO? When?
  - What did the RMO say about the PC?
  - Did the RMO say anything that indicated that there was any bias or animosity toward the Complainant for making the PC? Describe.
  - Do you believe that the RMO took the PA in reprisal for the Complainant making the PC? Why.
  - Do you believe the Complainant making the PC was a factor in the RMO taking the PA? Why?
  - Do you have any documents that relate to the PA? Provide.
- Ask individuals who recommended or influenced the PA:
  - What action did you recommend?
  - Why did you recommend the action?
  - Was the action you recommended the same as you have recommended in similar situations?
  - If no, why was it different?
  - Do you have any documents that relate to the PA? Provide.
- Ask the RMO:
  - Explain the circumstances that led you to take the PA involving the Complainant.
  - Why did you take the PA?
  - Who did you consult with in taking the PA?
  - Did anyone recommend or influence the PA?
  - If so, who, and what were the reasons they provided for recommending the PA?

- Have you taken the same action against others who did the same thing as the complainant?
- What was your reaction when you learned that the Complainant made the PC?
- Did the Complainant's PC influence your decision to take the PA?

5. Conducting Interviews

Ask open-ended questions. Avoid putting words in witnesses' mouths by asking questions like, "You really didn't reprise against CDR Smith, did you?" While leading a witness is inappropriate, summarizing a witness' testimony as you understand it is acceptable.

An interviewer might ask, "Was it your testimony that MAJ Smith's change of assignment was initiated by HRC?" This question clarifies previous testimony and is not a solicitation of new information.

a) **Beginning the Interview.** Investigators should use a standard read-in to begin an interview. Use a read-in provided by Service regulation or see sample read-in at Appendix D.

b) **Closing the Interview.** Investigators should use a standard read-out to conclude the interview. Either use a read-out provided under Service regulations, or see sample read-out at Appendix D.

6. Quality Assurance Review of Investigation

Upon completion of the fieldwork, investigators should perform a quality assurance review of their investigation using the checklist at Appendix E. The checklist is modeled after the oversight review worksheet used by the DoD OIG to review investigations. This affords the investigator an opportunity to perform a self-assessment of their investigation prior to submitting to the DoD OIG for approval.

The investigator should also go through the checklist after writing the report of investigation to double-check their work and to ensure that the quality standards for reports and supporting documentation are met.

SECTION 4. REPORTING REQUIREMENTS

1. Report of Investigation (ROI) - Format

The WRI ROI format includes an executive summary followed by sections on background, scope, statutory authority, findings of fact, analysis, discussion, conclusions, and recommendations, in that order (see Appendices F and G for WRI's 10 U.S.C. 1034 templates for reprisal and restriction, respectively).

a. Executive Summary

The Executive Summary should be a one-page section of the report designed to give the reader the most important information contained in the report in the most concise manner. The main elements of the Executive Summary are:

- **Introductory Paragraph.** The introductory paragraph should state that the investigation was conducted in response to allegations that the complainant suffered reprisal for making a protected communication. Start with: "We initiated this investigation in response to an allegation that [RMO name][2] took withheld or threatened to take or withhold action [replace "took withheld or threatened to take or withhold action" with the specific personnel action, such as, "did not recommend assignment extension," "denied an end-of-tour award"] to [complainant name] in reprisal for making a protected communication."
- **Findings Paragraph.** This paragraph should concisely summarize the factual findings related to the elements of reprisal.
- **Substantiation.** This paragraph should state whether or not the allegation was substantiated. It should include a clear description of the allegation that the RMO(s) did or did not take, withhold, or threaten to take the PA in question in reprisal for Complainant's protected communication(s), in violation of Title 10, United States Code, Section 1034 (10 U.S.C. 1034), "Protected communications; prohibition of retaliatory personnel actions," which is implemented by DoD Directive 7050.06, "Military Whistleblower Protection."

---

[2] Brackets are used throughout the examples to indicate the writer should insert information. Do not use the brackets in the ROI unless needed within a quote.

If there are multiple RMOs having different findings, summarize them separately as in the paragraph above; however, if they collectively took the actions, summarize them together.

- **Recommendation Paragraph.** In not substantiated cases, state, "We make no recommendations in this matter." In substantiated cases, state, "We recommend that the Secretary of the Military Department concerned:
  - Take appropriate corrective action regarding the [RMO name]; and
  - Specify here the relief to make the complainant whole; that is, to return the whistleblower, as nearly as practicable and reasonable, to the position the whistleblower would have held had the reprisal not occurred.

b. Background

This section should provide the reader information about the organizations, command relationships, and Complainant and management officials involved in the matter under investigation. Give a brief overview of events that led to the protected communication and personnel action. It may also be used to provide a very brief chronology or synopsis of key events leading up to the matters under investigation but generally not the matters directly under investigation. Do not include detailed narratives of the facts of the case that are presented in the Findings of Fact section of the report.

c. Scope

This section should describe the scope of the investigation in summary terms, leading with a statement of the timeframe addressed by the investigation, followed by key witnesses interviewed and crucial documents reviewed. Do not list every witness and every type of document. Include subject matter experts if their testimony was crucial to the outcome of the investigation.

d. Statutory Authority

The following statutory language should be cited:

> "The [name the investigating organization] conducted this whistleblower reprisal investigation pursuant to Title 10, United States Code, Section 1034 (10 U.S.C. 1034), "Protected communications; prohibition of retaliatory personnel actions," which is implemented by DoD Directive 7050.06, "Military Whistleblower Protection."

e. Findings of Fact

This section is a chronological telling of only the facts relevant to the case. State who, what, when, and where—without the use of terms such as protected communications, personnel actions, RMO knowledge, stated reason, RMO motive, animus, or disparate treatment. These terms are for analyzing what happened in relation to the elements of reprisal and should be reserved for the analysis section. Do not, for example, find that a visit to the IG is a protected communication or an unfavorable OER is a personnel action, or that an email to an RMO gave them knowledge of a protected communication etc.

Tell what happened, not the testimony about what happened. For facts not in dispute, state, for example, "Complainant told RMO during a meeting on September 11 that she had been sexually harassed by his XO," instead of "Complainant testified.... RMO testified..., etc."

Refer specifically to testimony or other evidence only where there are factual disputes in the testimony and resolve those discrepancies in this section. When this requires a credibility assessment, it should be done in this section as well.

f. Analysis

The analysis section begins with a standard paragraph describing the way reprisal is proven. This is to facilitate the understanding of the reader of the report. The paragraph states:

> The elements of reprisal are protected communication, knowledge of the protected communication on the part of the responsible management official; a personnel action taken, threatened, or withheld; and a causal connection between the protected communication and the personnel action. The causal connection is resolved by answering the question in paragraph D, below. If the evidence does not establish that the personnel action would have been taken, threatened, or withheld even absent the protected communication, then the complaint is substantiated. Conversely, if the evidence establishes that it would have been taken, threatened, or withheld absent the protected communication, then the complaint is not substantiated. Below, we analyze each of the elements.

This paragraph is followed by a subsection for each of the 4 elements to be analyzed—the headings are in the form of questions. The four-part analysis is a conjunctive standard; therefore, if one of the elements cannot be met (for example, if investigation reveals there was in fact no PC made or no RMO knowledge of the PC), it will ordinarily be unnecessary to address the subsequent elements. In those circumstances, following the last question analyzed, simply write, for example, "Because the RMO lacked knowledge of the PCs, reprisal could not have occurred."

The four questions to be addressed are as follows:

A. Did Complainant Make or Prepare to Make a Protected Communication, or Was Complainant Perceived As Having Made or Prepared to Make a Protected Communication?

Summarize the findings in the first sentence: "We determined that the Complainant made X protected communications and Y communications were not protected...."

Use a short paragraph for each alleged protected communication that synthesizes information already in the Findings of Fact section. Do not introduce new facts. This is merely listing each alleged protected communication and showing your determination that it either is or is not in fact a protected communication and why. These should not begin with "We found," or "So-and-so stated." They should end with a statement saying that an alleged protected communication is or is not protected under 10 U.S.C. 1034 and why.

When the investigation covers more than one protected communication, the first paragraph should summarize the different protected communications (not the facts for each protected communication) and serve as a topic paragraph for the section. Then use descriptive sub-headings to introduce a paragraph or more for each protected communication.

Conclude the entire section by stating, "As described above, a preponderance of the evidence established that Complainant ...."

B. Was an Unfavorable Personnel Action Taken or Threatened Against Complainant, or Was a Favorable Personnel Action Withheld or Threatened to Be Withheld from Complainant?

Summarize the findings in the first sentence: "We determined that Complainant was/was not the subject of [a personnel action]."

When the investigation covers only one personnel action, this paragraph should synthesize the facts related to the personnel action and determine whether or not it is a personnel action under the statute.

When the investigation covers more than one personnel action, the very first paragraph should summarize the different personnel actions (not the facts for each personnel action) and serve as a topic paragraph for the section. Then use descriptive sub-headings to introduce a paragraph for each personnel action.

Conclude the entire section by stating, "As described above, a preponderance of the evidence established that...."

C. Did the Responsible Management Official(s) Have Knowledge of Complainant's Protected Communication(s) or Perceive Complainant As Making or Preparing Protected Communication(S)?

Summarize the findings in the first sentence: "We determined that [RMO name] knew and [second RMO's name] perceived that Complainant had communicated with ..., and [third RMO's name] had no knowledge of any protected communications." Analyze in a separate paragraph or more the findings regarding each RMO.

The follow-on sentences/paragraphs should present the findings of fact—when each RMO first perceived or became aware of the protected communications(s). If knowledge by any RMO is undisputed, simply state the fact and cite the evidence establishing that fact (i.e., witness testimony, documentary evidence). If knowledge by any RMO is disputed, describe the evidence for and against knowledge and explain which is more compelling than the other—for example, the RMO may have stated that she had no knowledge, but a contemporaneous email discussing the protected communication establishes knowledge. Alternatively, you may need to make a credibility assessment of witnesses when you have competing testimony or weigh the authenticity of documentary evidence.

When the investigation covers more than one RMO or more than one PC, it may be appropriate to use descriptive sub-headings to organize this section to clearly present the relevant facts; you may choose to organize by RMO or by PC or some other approach, depending on the specifics of the case. In rare instances where the RMO was not interviewed, explain why.

Conclude the entire section by stating, "As described above, a preponderance of the evidence established that [RMO's name] knew and [second RMO's name] perceived that Complainant had communicated with .... [Third RMO's name] had no knowledge of the protected communications."

D. Would the Same Personnel Action(s) Have Been Taken, Withheld, or Threatened Absent the Protected Communication(s)? [Include D Only if Questions A-C Are All Answered in the Affirmative.]

Summarize the findings in the first sentence: "We determined that [RMO's name] would/would not have taken the personnel actions against Complainant absent his/her protected communications."

To determine the answer to this "causation" question, we must analyze what bearing, if any, the protected communication had on the decision to take, threaten, or withhold the personnel action. For each personnel action, we analyze the following factors:

- the strength of the evidence in support of the stated reason for the personnel action;
- the existence and strength of any motive to retaliate on the part of the agency officials who were involved in the decision; and
- any evidence that the similar actions have been taken against employees who are not whistleblowers, but who are otherwise similarly situated.

Do not retell the story already detailed in the findings of fact. Instead, refer to the events by the descriptive name given as the heading for each event, such as "September 1, 2013, Complaint to DoD Hotline" or "January 2013 email from DoD Hotline to [RMO's Name]."

For each personnel action, analyze the following factors and then weigh them together to determine whether the PA would have been taken absent the PC.

- Each RMO's stated reason(s) for the personnel action(s)

Remember, the fact that an action was within management's prerogative does not establish that the action would have been taken absent the PCs. Even if you find that the RMO(s) offered reasonable justification for the personnel action the investigation is not complete. The RMO(s) may offer that the action was taken based on the complainant's performance or conduct. The investigator must explore the possibility that others who did not make a PC but who have engaged in the same misconduct as the complainant were treated less harshly or not disciplined at all.

- Timing between the protected communication(s) and personnel action(s)

Dates of key events are usually of critical importance in the analysis of reprisal. This section should identify and analyze how much time elapsed between the PC(s) and PA(s). The closer the temporal proximity between the PC(s) and PA(s), the stronger the inference becomes of a possible causal connection between the events. Note that while an inference of causation is stronger when a PA is taken only a few days after a PC, a timing connection may still be present for lengthier gaps in time. For example, it is possible that the member's next performance evaluation was not due for nearly a year following the PC.

- Motive on the part of the RMO(s) to reprise

In this section, analyze the RMO's motive to reprise, including any animosity expressed by the RMO(s) regarding the protected communications. Did the complainant's protected communication allege any wrongdoing by any of the RMOs or otherwise implicate or criticize their performance, integrity, competence, or leadership? Have any of the RMOs exhibited or expressed animosity toward the very idea of, for example, filing an IG complaint or contacting a member of Congress?

- Disparate treatment of Complainant as compared to other similarly situated individuals who did not make PCs

How did the RMO(s) respond in the past to similarly situated personnel who did not make PCs? Are their actions in the case of the complainant consistent with past actions? If there is no evidence supporting a reason for handling the situation differently than in the past, it raises the inference of reprisal. If there is no evidence of similarly situated individuals, say so here.

Conclude the entire section by stating that, as described above, a preponderance of the evidence established [RMO's name] would or would not have taken, withheld, or threatened the specific personnel action in question absent the protected communication.

g. Discussion

Synthesize the analysis above in one or two paragraphs, explaining how we arrived at our conclusions. For example: "Based on a preponderance of the evidence, we conclude that [RMO name] issued an adverse OPR in reprisal for Complainant's protected communication to the IG. The evidence shows that Complainant's protected communication resulted in an investigation that substantiated misconduct by the RMO, who knew Complainant made the protected communication. [RMO name] told his XO and others that he was upset that Complainant went outside of the chain of command. Finally, the evidence shows that Complainant had received glowing OPR's prior to his protected communication, etc."

h. Conclusions

This section should provide a conclusion for each alleged PA addressed under the findings and analysis section of the report. The conclusion statement for each allegation should briefly identify the misconduct and the statute violated. For example:

> We conclude that General Morrow demoted Complainant in reprisal for contacting her congressional representative in violation of Title 10, United States Code, Section 1034.

i. Recommendations

If the complaint was substantiated, this section will recommend specific remedial actions to return the whistleblower, as nearly as practicable and reasonable, to the position the whistleblower would have held had the reprisal not occurred. Additionally, this section should include the general recommendation that appropriate action be taken against the RMO. For example:

We recommend that the Secretary of (the Service) direct [Service/Agency] officials to:

A. Remove Complainant's FITREP for (date) from his permanent record, and
B. Take appropriate corrective action against the RMO.

In cases where no corrective action is required, state that we make no recommendations.

2. Restriction Cases

Investigations into allegations of restriction require an answer to the question: "Did the RMO restrict the complainant from communicating with a member of Congress or an Inspector General?" Investigators must consider and analyze all of the evidence relating to the RMO's restriction (preventing or attempting to prevent a member of the Armed Forces from making or preparing to make a lawful communication to a member of Congress and/or an IG) of the complainant's access to a member of Congress or an Inspector General. It is not necessary for the RMO's attempt at restriction to be successful for such an allegation to be substantiated. ROIs on restriction cases follow a different template than that used for reprisal reports. See Appendix G for a restriction ROI template.

3. Reporting When the Case Cannot be Completed within 180 Days

If, in the course of an investigation, it becomes clear that the report cannot be issued within 180 days of the filing of the complaint, the responsible Inspector General shall notify the complainant, in writing, of the reasons for the delay and when the report will be issued. The same information must be sent to the Deputy Under Secretary of Defense for Personnel and Readiness; IG DoD, Whistleblower Reprisal Investigations Directorate; the Secretary of the military department concerned; and the member or former member; this can be accomplished by courtesy-copying them the letter to the Complainant (See Appendix H for a sample letter).

4. Reporting Closed Cases

Within 30 days after Whistleblower Reprisal Investigations Directorate approves the ROI or the determination that an investigation is not warranted, the Service IG must send a letter to the complainant informing him or her (1) of the investigative findings, (2) that a copy of the report on the results of the investigation is enclosed, and (3) of the right to appeal to the appropriate BCMR (see Appendix I for a sample letter). The report must contain the maximum disclosure of information that is possible, except for information that may be withheld under the Freedom of Information and Privacy Acts. The letter must be courtesy-copied to the:

- Deputy Under Secretary of Defense for Personnel and Readiness,
- DoD IG Directorate for Whistleblower Reprisal Investigations,
- relevant Board for Corrections of Military Records, and
- Secretary of the military department concerned.

Appendix List

A. Title 10, United States Code, Section 1034, "Protected communications; prohibition of retaliatory actions," and DoD Directive 7050.06, "Military Whistleblower Protection."
B. Complaint Intake Form.
C. Military Reprisal Investigative Plan.
D. Interview Read In/Read Out.
E. IO Checklist.
F. WRI 1034 Reprisal ROI Template.
G. WRI Restriction ROI Template.
H. 180-day letter to the complainant.
I. Closure letter to the complainant.

10 U.S.C.

ARMED FORCES Subtitle A - General

Military Law PART II - PERSONNEL

CHAPTER 53 - MISCELLANEOUS RIGHTS AND BENEFITS

Sec. 1034 - Protected communications; prohibition of retaliatory personnel actions

§1034. Protected communications; prohibition of retaliatory personnel actions

(a) Restricting Communications With Members of Congress and Inspector General Prohibited.—

(1) No person may restrict a member of the armed forces in communicating with a Member of Congress or an Inspector General.

(2) Paragraph (1) does not apply to a communication that is unlawful.

(b) Prohibition of Retaliatory Personnel Actions.—

(1) No person may take (or threaten to take) an unfavorable personnel action, or withhold (or threaten to withhold) a favorable personnel action, as a

reprisal against a member of the armed forces for making or preparing or being perceived as making or preparing—

(A) a communication to a Member of Congress or an Inspector General that (under subsection (a)) may not be restricted;

(B) a communication that is described in subsection (c)(2) and that is made (or prepared to be made) to—

(i) a Member of Congress;

(ii) an Inspector General (as defined in subsection (i)) or any other Inspector General appointed under the Inspector General Act of 1978;

(iii) a member of a Department of Defense audit, inspection, investigation, or law enforcement organization;

(iv) any person or organization in the chain of command;

(v) a court-martial proceeding; or

(vi) any other person or organization designated pursuant to regulations or other established administrative procedures for such communications; or

(C) testimony, or otherwise participating in or assisting in an investigation or proceeding related to a communication under subparagraph (A) or (B), or filing, causing to be filed, participating in, or otherwise assisting in an action brought under this section.

(2) Any action prohibited by paragraph (1) (including the threat to take any unfavorable action, or making or threatening to make a significant change in the duties or responsibilities of a member of the armed forces not commensurate with the member's grade, and the withholding or threat to withhold any favorable action) shall be considered for the purposes of this section to be a personnel action prohibited by this subsection.

(c) Inspector General Investigation of Allegations of Prohibited Personnel Actions.—

(1) If a member of the armed forces submits to an Inspector General an allegation that a personnel action prohibited by subsection (b) has been taken (or threatened) against the member with respect to a communication described in paragraph (2), the Inspector General shall take the action required under paragraph (4).

(2) A communication described in this paragraph is a communication in which a member of the armed forces complains of, or discloses information that the member reasonably believes constitutes evidence of, any of the following:

(A) A violation of law or regulation, including a law or regulation prohibiting rape, sexual assault, or other sexual misconduct in violation of sections 920 through 920c of this title (articles 120 through 120c of the

Uniformed Code of Military Justice), sexual harassment or unlawful discrimination.

(B) Gross mismanagement, a gross waste of funds, an abuse of authority, or a substantial and specific danger to public health or safety.

(C) A threat by another member of the armed forces or employee of the Federal Government that indicates a determination or intent to kill or cause serious bodily injury to members of the armed forces or civilians or damage to military, Federal, or civilian property.

(3) A communication described in paragraph (2) shall not be excluded from the protections provided in this section because—

(A) the communication was made to a person who participated in an activity that the member reasonably believed to be covered by paragraph (2);

(B) the communication revealed information that had been previously disclosed;

(C) of the member's motive for making the communication;

(D) the communication was not made in writing;

(E) the communication was made while the member was off duty: and

(F) the communication was made during the normal course of duties of the member.

(4)(A) An Inspector General receiving an allegation as described in paragraph (1) shall expeditiously determine, in accordance with regulations prescribed under subsection (h), whether there is sufficient evidence to warrant an investigation of the allegation.

(B) If the Inspector General receiving such an allegation is an Inspector General within a military department, that Inspector General shall promptly notify the Inspector General of the Department of Defense of the allegation. Such notification shall be made in accordance with regulations prescribed under subsection (h).

(C) If an allegation under paragraph (1) is submitted to an Inspector General within a military department and if the determination of that Inspector General under subparagraph (A) is that there is not sufficient evidence to warrant an investigation of the allegation, that Inspector General shall forward the matter to the Inspector General of the Department of Defense for review.

(D) Upon determining that an investigation of an allegation under paragraph (1) is warranted, the Inspector General making the determination shall expeditiously investigate the allegation. In the case of a determination made by the Inspector General of the Department of Defense, that Inspector General may delegate responsibility for the investigation to an appropriate Inspector General within a military department.

(E) In the case of an investigation under subparagraph (D) within the Department of Defense, the results of the investigation shall be determined by, or approved by, the Inspector General of the Department of Defense (regardless of whether the investigation itself is conducted by the Inspector General of the Department of Defense or by an Inspector General within a military department).

(5) Neither an initial determination under paragraph (3)(A) nor an investigation under paragraph (3)(D) is required in the case of an allegation made more than one year after the date on which the member becomes aware of the personnel action that is the subject of the allegation.

(6) The Inspector General of the Department of Defense, or the Inspector General of the Department of Homeland Security (in the case of a member of the Coast Guard when the Coast Guard is not operating as a service in the Navy), shall ensure that the Inspector General conducting the investigation of an allegation under this subsection is one or both of the following:

(A) Outside the immediate chain of command of both the member submitting the allegation and the individual or individuals alleged to have taken the retaliatory action.

(B) At least one organization higher in the chain of command than the organization of the member submitting the allegation and the individual or individuals alleged to have taken the retaliatory action.

(d) Inspector General Investigation of Underlying Allegations.—Upon receiving an allegation under subsection (c), the Inspector General receiving the allegation shall conduct a separate investigation of the information that the member making the allegation believes constitutes evidence of wrongdoing (as described in subparagraph (A), (B), or (C) of subsection (c)(2)) if there previously has not been such an investigation or if the Inspector General determines that the original investigation was biased or otherwise inadequate. In the case of an allegation received by the Inspector General of the Department of Defense, the Inspector General may delegate that responsibility to the Inspector General of the armed force concerned.

(e) Reports on Investigations.—

(1) After completion of an investigation under subsection (c) or (d) or, in the case of an investigation under subsection (c) by an Inspector General within a military department, after approval of the report of that investigation under subsection (c)(4)(E), the Inspector General conducting the investigation shall submit a report on the results of the investigation to the Secretary of Defense and the Secretary of the military department concerned (or to the Secretary of Homeland Security in the case of a member of the Coast Guard

when the Coast Guard is not operating as a service in the Navy) and shall transmit a copy of the report on the results of the investigation to the member of the armed forces who made the allegation investigated. The report shall be transmitted to such Secretaries, and the copy of the report shall be transmitted to the member, not later than 30 days after the completion of the investigation or, in the case of an investigation under subsection (c) by an Inspector General within a military department, after approval of the report of that investigation under subsection (c)(4)(E).

(2) In the copy of the report transmitted to the member, the Inspector General shall ensure the maximum disclosure of information possible, with the exception of information that is not required to be disclosed under section 552 of title 5. However, the copy need not include summaries of interviews conducted, nor any document acquired, during the course of the investigation. Such items shall be transmitted to the member, if the member requests the items, with the copy of the report or after the transmittal to the member of the copy of the report, regardless of whether the request for those items is made before or after the copy of the report is transmitted to the member.

(3) If, in the course of an investigation of an allegation under this section, the Inspector General determines that it is not possible to submit the report required by paragraph (1) within 180 days after the date of receipt of the allegation being investigated, the Inspector General shall provide to the Secretary of Defense and the Secretary of the military department concerned (or to the Secretary of Homeland Security in the case of a member of the Coast Guard when the Coast Guard is not operating as a service in the Navy) and to the member making the allegation a notice—

(A) of that determination (including the reasons why the report may not be submitted within that time); and

(B) of the time when the report will be submitted.

(4) The report on the results of the investigation shall contain a thorough review of the facts and circumstances relevant to the allegation and the complaint or disclosure and shall include documents acquired during the course of the investigation, including summaries of interviews conducted. The report may include a recommendation as to the disposition of the complaint.

(f) Action in case of violations—

(1) Not later than 30 days after receiving a report from the Inspector General under subsection (e), the Secretary of Homeland Security or the Secretary of the military department concerned, as applicable, shall determine whether there is sufficient basis to conclude whether a personnel action prohibited by subsection (b) has occurred.

(2) If the Secretary concerned determines under paragraph (1) that a personnel action prohibited by section (b) has occurred, the Secretary shall—

(A) order such action as is necessary to correct the record of a personnel action prohibited by subsection (b); and

(B) take any appropriate disciplinary action against the individual who committed such prohibited personnel action.

(3) If the Secretary concerned determines under paragraph (1) that an order for corrective or disciplinary action is not appropriate, not later than 30 days after making the determination, such Secretary shall—

(A) provide to the Secretary of Defense and the member or former member a notice of the determination and the reasons for not taking action; and

(B) when appropriate, refer the report to the appropriate board for the correction of military records for further review under subsection (g).

(g) Correction of Records When Prohibited Action Taken.—

(1) A board for the correction of military records acting under section 1552 of this title, in resolving an application for the correction of records made by a member or former member of the armed forces who has alleged a personnel action prohibited by subsection (b), on the request of the member or former member or otherwise, may review the matter.

(2) In resolving an application described in paragraph (1), a correction board—

(A) shall review the report of the Inspector General submitted under subsection (e)(1);

(B) may request the Inspector General to gather further evidence; and

(C) may receive oral argument, examine and cross-examine witnesses, take depositions, and, if appropriate, conduct an evidentiary hearing.

(3) If the board holds an administrative hearing, the member or former member who filed the application described in paragraph (1)—

(A) may be provided with representation by a judge advocate if—

(i) the Inspector General, in the report under subsection (e)(1), finds that there is probable cause to believe that a personnel action prohibited by subsection (b) has been taken (or threatened) against the member with respect to a communication described in subsection (c)(2);

(ii) the Judge Advocate General concerned determines that the member or former member would benefit from judge advocate assistance to ensure proper presentation of the legal issues in the case; and

(iii) the member is not represented by outside counsel chosen by the member; and

(B) may examine witnesses through deposition, serve interrogatories, and request the production of evidence, including evidence contained in the investigatory record of the Inspector General but not included in the report submitted under subsection (e)(1).

(4) The Secretary concerned shall issue a final decision with respect to an application described in paragraph (1) within 180 days after the application is filed. If the Secretary fails to issue such a final decision within that time, the member or former member shall be deemed to have exhausted the member's or former member's administrative remedies under section 1552 of this title.

(5) The Secretary concerned shall order such action, consistent with the limitations contained in sections 1552 and 1553 of this title, as is necessary to correct the record of a personnel action prohibited by subsection (b).

(6) If the Board determines that a personnel action prohibited by subsection (b) has occurred, the Board may recommend to the Secretary concerned that the Secretary take appropriate disciplinary action against the individual who committed such personnel action.

(h) Review by Secretary of Defense.—Upon the completion of all administrative review under subsection (f), the member or former member of the armed forces (except for a member or former member of the Coast Guard when the Coast Guard is not operating as a service in the Navy) who made the allegation referred to in subsection (c)(1), if not satisfied with the disposition of the matter, may submit the matter to the Secretary of Defense. The Secretary shall make a decision to reverse or uphold the decision of the Secretary of the military department concerned in the matter within 90 days after receipt of such a submittal.

(i) Regulations.—The Secretary of Defense, and the Secretary of Homeland Security with respect to the Coast Guard when it is not operating as a service in the Navy, shall prescribe regulations to carry out this section.

(k) Definitions.—In this section:

(1) The term "Member of Congress" includes any Delegate or Resident Commissioner to Congress.

(2) The term "Inspector General" means any of the following:

(A) The Inspector General of the Department of Defense.

(B) The Inspector General of the Department of Homeland Security, in the case of a member of the Coast Guard when the Coast Guard is not operating as a service in the Navy.

(C) Any officer of the armed forces or employee of the Department of Defense who is assigned or detailed to serve as an Inspector General at any level in the Department of Defense.

(3) The term "unlawful discrimination" means discrimination on the basis of race, color, religion, sex, or national origin.

DEPARTMENT OF DEFENSE DIRECTIVE

NUMBER 7050.06
April 17, 2015

IG DoD

SUBJECT: Military Whistleblower Protection
References: See Enclosure 1

1. PURPOSE. This directive reissues DoD Directive (DoDD) 7050.06 (Reference (a)) to update established policies and assigned responsibilities for military whistleblower protection pursuant to section 1034 of Title 10, United States Code (U.S.C.) (Reference (b)).

2. APPLICABILITY. This directive applies to OSD, the Military Departments, the Office of the Chairman of the Joint Chiefs of Staff and the Joint Staff, the Combatant Commands, the Defense Agencies, the DoD Field Activities, and all other organizational entities within the DoD (referred to collectively in this directive as the "DoD Components") and the Office of the Inspector General of the Department of Defense (IG DoD).

3. POLICY. It is DoD policy that:

a. Members of the Military Services (referred to in this directive as "Service members") are free to make protected communications.

b. No person will restrict a Service member from making lawful communications to a member of Congress or an inspector general (IG).

c. Service members will be free from reprisal for making or preparing to make or being perceived as making or preparing to make a protected communication.

d. No person may take or threaten to take an unfavorable personnel action or withhold or threaten to withhold a favorable personnel action in reprisal against any Service member for making or preparing to make, or being perceived as making or preparing to make a protected communication.

e. No investigation is required when a Service member (hereinafter, use of "Service member" includes both current and former Service members) submits a reprisal complaint more than 1 year after the date that the member became aware of the personnel action that is the subject of the allegation. However, an IG receiving a reprisal complaint more than 1 year later may consider the complaint based on compelling reasons or circumstances. These circumstances may include situations in which the Service member:

(1) Was actively misled regarding his or her rights;

(2) Was prevented in some extraordinary way from exercising his or her rights; or

(3) Filed the same allegation within the 1 year period with the wrong office or agency.

4. RESPONSIBILITIES. See Enclosure 2.

5. RELEASABILITY. **Cleared for public release.**. This directive is available on the Internet from the DoD Issuances Website at http://www.dtic.mil/whs/directives.

6. EFFECTIVE DATE. This directive is effective on April 17, 2015.

Robert O. Work
Deputy Secretary of Defense

Enclosures

1. References
2. Responsibilities
Glossary

Enclosure 1

References

a) DoD Directive 7050.06, "Military Whistleblower Protection," July 23, 2007 (hereby cancelled)
b) Title 10, United States Code
c) Title 5, United States Code
d) DoD Directive 5505.06, "Investigations of Allegations Against Senior DoD Officials," June 6, 2013
e) DoD Directive 5106.04, "Defense Inspectors General," May 22, 2014

f) DoD Instruction 6490.04, "Mental Health Evaluations of Members of the Military Services," March 4, 2013

Enclosure 2

Responsibilities

Unless otherwise expressly provided below, the responsibilities in this enclosure may be delegated in writing.

1. IG DoD. The IG DoD investigates or oversees DoD Component IG investigations of allegations that the prohibitions of restriction or reprisal of this directive have been violated. To ensure compliance with this directive and section 1034 of Reference (b), the IG DoD:

a. Determines if there is sufficient evidence to warrant an investigation of an allegation submitted to the IG DoD by a Service member that the prohibitions of restriction or reprisal have been violated. Within 30 days after the date of receipt of a complaint with sufficient evidence to warrant further investigation, IG DoD initiates an investigation or requests the DoD Component IG to initiate an investigation.

b. Reviews determinations by DoD Component IGs that investigation of an allegation is not warranted. Notifies the DoD Component IG of approval or concerns.

c. Ensures the investigating DoD Component IG:

(1) Is outside the immediate chain of command (as established under DoD Component regulations) of both the Service member submitting the allegation and the individual or individuals alleged to have taken the retaliatory action; or

(2) Is at least one organization higher in the chain of command than the organization of the Service member submitting the allegation and the individual or individuals alleged to have taken the retaliatory action.

d. Reviews the results of investigations into violations of restrictions and reprisals conducted by DoD Component IGs. Approves the results or ensures the DoD Component IG corrects inadequacies or initiates a follow-up investigation. Notifies DoD Component IG of approval.

e. Reports the results of the IG DoD investigation within 180 days after the date of receipt of an allegation of reprisal or restriction. The report will include:

(1) A thorough review of the facts and circumstances relevant to the allegation(s), relevant documents acquired during the course of investigation, and summaries or transcripts of interviews conducted.

(2) Recommendations for an appropriate remedy for the whistleblower in a substantiated case.

f. If a report of the IG DoD investigation cannot be issued within 180 days, notifies the Under Secretary of Defense for Personnel and Readiness (USD(P&R)), the Secretary of the Military Department concerned, and the Service member of the reasons for the delay and of the time when the report will be issued.

g. Conducts or requests a DoD Component IG to conduct a separate investigation of the underlying allegations contained in the protected communication when:

(1) An investigation has not been initiated; or

(2) An investigation of the allegation(s) contained in the protected communication has been conducted, and the IG DoD determines that the investigation was biased or inadequate.

h. Maintains reports on the results of the IG DoD investigation of restriction, reprisal, or underlying allegations and is responsible for transmitting the reports to the USD(P&R), the Secretary of the Military Department concerned, and the Service member not later than 30 days after the completion of the investigation; and when requested, transmits a copy of the documents acquired during the investigation and summaries or transcripts of testimony to the Service member. Ensures the copy of the report and supporting documents released to the Service member includes the maximum disclosure of information possible, with the exception of information that is not required to be disclosed in accordance with section 552 of Title 5, U.S.C. (Reference (c)).

i. Advises the Service member concerned that he or she may request review of the matter by a Board for Correction of Military Records (BCMR).

j. At the request of a BCMR, submits a copy of the report on the results of the investigation and gathers further evidence.

2. USD(P&R). On behalf of the Secretary of Defense, the USD(P&R):

a. Reviews reports on the results of investigations conducted pursuant to this directive and section 1034 of Reference (b).

b. Within 90 days of receipt of an appeal of a decision pursuant to this directive:

(1) Reviews the final decision of the Secretary of the Military Department concerned on applications for correction of military records decided in accordance with this directive and section 1034 of Reference (b).

(2) Decides whether to uphold or reverse the decision of the Secretary of the Military Department concerned. The decision of the USD(P&R) is final within the Department of Defense.

c. If necessary, requests the Secretary of the Military Department concerned comment on evidence considered by a BCMR when the Secretary of Defense is requested to reconsider the final decision of the Secretary of the Military Department concerned.

d. Notifies the IG DoD and Military Department IG concerned of decisions made on appeals pursuant to this directive to the Secretary of Defense.

3. DoD COMPONENT HEADS. The DoD Component heads:

a. Will maintain regulations governing civilian employees that makes any violation of the prohibitions of restriction and reprisal the basis for appropriate disciplinary action.

b. Direct that all allegations submitted in accordance with section 1034 of Reference (b) are thoroughly, objectively, and timely considered, and appropriate corrective actions are taken.

c. Direct that their respective IGs:

(1) Establish internal procedures for receiving, reporting, and investigating pursuant to this directive and section 1034 of Reference (b) allegations that the prohibitions of restriction and reprisal have been violated.

(2) Notify the IG DoD within 10 working days after receiving any allegation that the prohibitions of restriction or reprisal of this directive have been violated. Provide a copy of the written complaint to the IG DoD.

(3) Determine if there is sufficient evidence to warrant an investigation within 30 days of receipt of a restriction or reprisal allegation.

(4) Forward to the IG DoD any determination that there is not sufficient evidence to warrant investigation. If the IG DoD agrees with the determination, the DoD Component IG will notify the Service member making the allegation.

(5) Initiate an investigation when it has been determined investigation is warranted or upon the request of IG DoD. Forward reports on the results of investigation to the IG DoD for approval.

(6) Apply the provisions of DoDD 5505.06 (Reference (d)) when a reprisal or restriction allegation is made against a senior official of the DoD.

d. Ensure the investigating IG:

(1) Is outside the immediate chain of command (as established under DoD Component regulations) of both the Service member submitting the allegation(s) and the individual(s) alleged to have taken the retaliatory action; or

(2) Is at least one organization higher in the chain of command than the organization of the Service member submitting the allegation and the individual or individuals alleged to have taken the retaliatory action.

e. Provide the IG DoD with the report of investigation within 150 days after the date of receipt of the allegation from the Service member by the DoD Component IG or IG DoD. Include in the report:

(1) A thorough review of the facts and circumstances relevant to the allegation(s), relevant documents acquired during the investigation, and summaries or transcripts of interviews conducted.

(2) Recommendations for an appropriate remedy for the whistleblower in a substantiated case.

f. If the report cannot be issued within 180 days after receipt of the allegation, notify the USD(P&R), IG DoD, the Secretary of the Military Department concerned, and the Service member of the reasons for the delay and an estimate of when the report will be issued.

g. Conduct a separate investigation of the underlying allegations contained in the protected communication when an investigation has not been initiated or an investigation of the allegation(s) contained in the protected communication has been conducted, and the DoD Component IG or IG DoD determines that the investigation was biased or inadequate.

h. Transmit a report on the results of the investigation of restriction, reprisal, or underlying allegations to the USD(P&R), the Secretary of the Military Department concerned, and the Service member not later than 30 days after IG DoD approval of the results of the investigation. If requested, transmit a copy of the documents acquired during the investigation and summaries or transcripts of testimony to the Service member. Ensure the copy of the report and supporting documents released to the Service member includes the maximum disclosure of information possible, with the exception of information not required to be disclosed pursuant to section 552 of Reference (c).

i. Advise the Service member that he or she may request review of the matter by a BCMR.

j. At the request of a BCMR, ensures the investigating IG submits a copy of the investigation report or gathers further evidence.

k. Ensure that the subject(s) of the investigation of an allegation of restriction or reprisal conducted in accordance with this directive are afforded procedural protections, including the opportunity to present matters on their behalf, incident to administrative or disciplinary action, under DoD Component regulations or other established administrative procedures governing such action.

l. Publicize the content of this directive to ensure that members of the Military Services and other DoD personnel fully understand its scope and application.

4. SECRETARIES OF THE MILITARY DEPARTMENTS. In addition to the responsibilities in section 3 of this enclosure, the Secretaries of the Military Departments:

a. Will maintain regulations that make punishable, under Article 92 of Chapter 47 of Reference (b) (also known and referred to in this directive as "the Uniform Code of Military Justice (UCMJ)"), any violation of the prohibitions of restriction and reprisal by persons subject to the UCMJ.

b. Not later than 30 days after receiving a report from or approved by IG DoD of a substantiated allegation, determine if there is sufficient basis to conclude the prohibition of restriction or reprisal of this directive has been violated.

c. When a prohibition has been violated:

(1) Order the record of the Service member corrected.

(2) Take any appropriate disciplinary or corrective action against the individual who committed the restriction or reprisal.

d. If an order for remedial, disciplinary, or corrective action is not appropriate, not later than 30 days after making the determination:

(1) Provide the Secretary of Defense and the Service member a notice of the determination and the reasons for not taking action.

(2) When appropriate, refer the report to the appropriate BCMR for further review.

e. Based on the IG report, take remedial action including assisting members in preparing an application to BCMR when implementation of the recommendations of the report requires action by a BCMR. Notify IG DoD of remedial action taken within 10 working days of taking action.

f. Ensure their respective BCMRs:

(1) Considers applications for the correction of military records at the request of a Service member who alleged restriction or reprisal.

(2) Establishes procedures to resolve such an application that as a minimum include:

(a) Reviewing the IG report submitted to the Secretary of the Military Department concerned.

(b) Requesting the IG DoD or the Military Department IG concerned to gather further evidence if needed.

(c) As appropriate, taking depositions, conducting an evidentiary hearing, examining and cross-examining witnesses, and receiving oral arguments.

(d) As appropriate, recommending to the Secretary of the Military Department concerned that disciplinary action be taken against the individual responsible for violations of the prohibitions.

(e) If the BCMR holds a hearing, the Service member who filed the application:

1. May be provided with representation by a judge advocate if:

a. The IG investigation finds the prohibition of reprisal has been violated.

b. The Judge Advocate General concerned determines that the Service member would benefit from judge advocate assistance to ensure proper presentation of the legal issues in the case.

c. The Service member is not represented by outside counsel.

2. The Service member may examine witnesses through depositions, serve interrogatories, and request the production of evidence, including evidence in an IG investigative record not included in the report released to the Service member.

g. Issue a final decision on an application submitted to the BCMR in accordance with this directive within 180 days after the application is filed. If the Secretary of the Military Department fails to issue a final decision within that time, the Service member will be deemed to have exhausted the administrative remedies afforded by section 1552 of Reference (b).

h. Advise the Service member that he or she may request review of the matter by the USD(P&R) on behalf of the Secretary of Defense. The request must be made within 90 days after receipt of the Secretary of the Military Department's decision.

i. Order such action, consistent with the limitations in section 1552 and 1553 of Reference (b), to correct the record of a personnel action prohibited by section 1034 of Reference (b).

j. Notify the IG DoD, the USD(P&R), and the Military Department IG concerned of a decision on an application for the correction of military records received from a Service member pursuant to this directive.

GLOSSARY

Part I. Abbreviations and Acronyms

BCMR	Board for Correction of Military Records
DoDD	DoD Directive
IG	inspector general
IG DoD	Inspector General of the Department of Defense
UCMJ	Uniform Code of Military Justice
U.S.C.	United States Code
USD(P&R)	Under Secretary of Defense for Personnel and Readiness

Part II. Definitions

Unless otherwise noted, these definitions are for the purposes of this directive.

abuse of authority. An arbitrary or capricious exercise of power by a military member or a federal official or employee that adversely affects the rights of any person or results in personal gain or advantage to himself or herself or to preferred other persons.

audit, inspection, investigation, or law enforcement organizations. The IG DoD, the U.S. Army Audit Agency, the Naval Audit Service, the Air Force Audit Agency, and the Defense Contract Audit Agency. The law enforcement organizations at any command level in any of the DoD Components, the Defense Criminal Investigative Service, the U.S. Army Criminal Investigation Command, the Naval Criminal Investigative Service, and the Air Force Office of Special Investigations.

BCMR. Any board empowered pursuant to section 1552 of Reference (b) to recommend correction of military records to the Secretary of the Military Department concerned.

chain of command. The succession of commanding officers from a superior to a subordinate through which command is exercised; also the succession of officers, enlisted members, or civilian personnel through whom administrative control is exercised, including supervision and rating of performance. For members of the National Guard this also includes the Adjutant General and the Governor of the State.

gross mismanagement. A management action or inaction that creates a substantial risk of significant adverse impact on the agency's ability to accomplish its mission. The matter must be significant and more than *de minimis* wrongdoing or simple negligence. It does not include management decisions that are merely debatable among reasonable people.

gross waste of funds. An expenditure that is significantly out of proportion to the benefit reasonably expected to accrue to the government.

IGs. The IG DoD; the Military Department IGs (these include the Military Department IGs and IGs assigned or detailed under regulations of the Secretary of the Military Department concerned to serve at any command level in one of the Military Services); Defense IGs (as defined in DoDD 5106.04 (Reference (e)); an IG appointed under Appendix of Reference (c).

member of Congress. A U.S. Senator or Representative, delegate or resident Commissioner to the U.S. Congress, or a staff member of a Senator, Representative, or congressional committee, delegate, or resident Commissioner.

personnel action. Any action taken on a Service member that affects, or has the potential to affect, that member's current position or career. Such actions include promotion; disciplinary or other corrective action; transfer or reassignment; a performance evaluation; decisions concerning pay, benefits, awards, or training, relief and removal; separation; discharge; referral for mental health evaluations in accordance with DoD Instruction 6490.04 (Reference (f)); and any other significant change in duties or responsibilities inconsistent with the Service member's grade.

protected communication. The Table describes when a communication is protected.

remedial action. Appropriate relief to make the complainant whole, to include such action as is necessary to correct the record of a retaliatory personnel action.

reprisal. Taking or threatening to take an unfavorable personnel action, or withholding or threatening to withhold a favorable personnel action, for making, preparing to make, or being perceived as making or preparing to make a protected communication.

restriction. Preventing or attempting to prevent a current Service member from making or preparing to make a lawful communication to a member of Congress or an IG.

Service member. A Regular or Reserve Component officer (commissioned and warrant) or enlisted member of the Army, the Navy, the Air Force, the Marine Corps, and the Coast Guard (when it is operating as a

Service in the Navy) on active duty. A Reserve Component officer (commissioned and warrant) or enlisted member in any duty or training status, including officers and enlisted members of the National Guard.

unlawful discrimination. Discrimination on the basis of race, color, religion, sex, or national origin.

whistleblower. A Service member who makes, prepares to make, or is perceived as making or preparing to make a protected communication.

Table. Protected Communication

Type of Communication:	Conditions on Protection:	When made to:
Any communication	Must be a lawful communication	• A member of Congress or • An IG
Any communication in which a Service member communicates information that he or she reasonably believes evidences: • A violation of law or regulation, including a law or regulation prohibiting rape, sexual assault, or other sexual misconduct in violations of section 920 through 920c of Reference (c) (articles 120 through 120c of the UCMJ), sexual harassment or unlawful discrimination; • Gross mismanagement, a gross waste of funds or other resources, an abuse of authority, or a substantial and specific danger to public health or safety; or	A communication will not lose its protected status because: • The communication was made to a person who participated in the activity that the Service member complained of; • The communication revealed information that had been previously disclosed; • Of the Service member's motive for making the communication; • The communication was not in writing; • The communication was made while the Service member was off duty; or • The communication was made during the normal course of the Service member's duties.	• A member of Congress; • An IG; • A member of a DoD audit, inspection, investigation, or law enforcement organization; • Any person or organization in the chain of command; • A court-martial proceeding; or • Any other person or organization designated pursuant to regulations or other established administrative procedures to receive such communications.

Table. (Continued)

Type of Communication:	Conditions on Protection:	When made to:
• A threat by another Service member or employee of the Federal Government that indicates a determination or intent to kill or cause serious bodily injury to Service members or civilians or damage to military, federal, or civilian property. • Testimony, or otherwise participating in or assisting in an investigation or proceeding related to a communication as described above; or • Filing, or causing to be filed, participating in, or otherwise assisting in a military whistleblower reprisal action.		

APPENDIX B
MILITARY REPRISAL COMPLAINT INTAKE WORKSHEET

Case Number:
Investigator:
Complainant:
Date Complaint Filed:
Filed within 1 year of most recent PA? Yes/No

Statutory Authority: Title 10, United States Code, Section 1034 (10 U.S.C. 1034), "Protected communications; prohibition of retaliatory personnel actions," as implemented by DoD Directive 7050.06, "Military Whistleblower Protection."

Case Summary:

Element 1: Did Complainant make or prepare to make a protected communication (PC), or was Complainant perceived as making or preparing a protected communication?

10 U.S.C. 1034 "PROTECTED COMMUNICATION; PROHIBITION OF RETALIATORY PERSONNEL ACTIONS" DoD Directive 7050.06, "Military Whistleblower Protection"	(a) PROHIBITION OF RESTRICTION		
	No person may restrict a member of the armed forces in lawfully communicating with a Member of Congress or an IG.		
	(b) PROHIBITION OF RETALIATORY PERSONNEL ACTIONS		
	PROTECTED COMMUNICATION	TO	PERSONNEL ACTIONS
	(b)(1) Making or preparing or being perceived as making or preparing: (A) Any lawful communication to a Member of Congress or an Inspector General (IG) (B) Information reasonably believed to evidence: • A violation of law or regulation, including a law or regulation prohibiting rape, sexual assault, or other sexual misconduct in violation of articles 120 through 120c of the UCMJ, sexual harassment or unlawful discrimination. • Gross mismanagement, a gross waste of funds, an abuse of authority, or a substantial and specific danger to public health or safety. • A threat that indicates a member's or federal employee's determination or intent to kill or cause serious bodily injury to members or civilians or damage to military, federal or civilian property (C) • Testifying or participating in or assisting in an investigation or proceeding related to a PC • Filing, causing to be filed, participating in, or otherwise assisting in an action under this section	(b)(1) (A) Member of Congress or Inspector General (B) • Member of a Department of Defense audit, inspection, investigation, or law enforcement organization • Any person or organization in the chain of command • A court-martial proceeding • Any other person or organization designated pursuant to regulations or other established administrative procedures for such communications.	• Taking an unfavorable personnel action • Threatening to take an unfavorable personnel action • Withholding a favorable personnel action • Threatening to withhold a favorable personnel action • Making or threatening to make a significant change in the duties or responsibilities of a member of the armed forces not commensurate with the member's grade DoDD 7050.06: Any action that affects, or has the potential to affect, the military member's current position or career, including: • Promotions • Disciplinary/corrective actions • Performance evaluations • Decisions on pay, benefits, awards, training • Referrals for Mental Health Evaluation

Military Reprisal Complaint Intake Worksheet

Alleged PC #1: ***(add more as needed)***
Description:

To whom:
Date:
Determination: Protected/Not Protected

Element 2: Was an unfavorable personnel action (PA) taken or threatened against Complainant, or was a favorable personnel action withheld or threatened to be withheld from Complainant?

Alleged PA #1: ***(add more as needed)***
Action:

By whom? (Responsible Management Official (RMO)):

Were there other individuals involved in recommending, approving, or influencing the PA?

Date:

Determination: PA/Not PA

Possible Inference of Knowledge? Yes/No
Explain:

Knowledge Questions to ask Complainant:

- Did the RMO have knowledge of the PC or suspect you?
- What, if anything, was done in response to your PC(s)?
- How much time passed between your PC(s) and the PA(s) taken against you?

Possible Inference of Causation: Yes/No
Explain:

Causation Questions to ask Complainant:

- Why do you believe the action taken, withheld, or threatened was in reprisal?
- What motive would the RMO have to reprise against you?
- What were the reasons provided to you by the RMO for the action they took?

Prima Facie Allegation? Yes/No

Recommendation: Dismiss/Investigate

Inference of Causation: Does the complaint, as supplemented by an interview of the complainant support an inference of reprisal—that is, a causal connection between the PC and the PA? This can be met where the facts suggest the existence of one or more of the following:

- The PA followed closely behind the PC
- The PC was about something that would give the RMO motive to reprise
- The RMO expressed animosity toward the Complainant and/or the PC
- The Complainant received worse treatment than others in similar situations who have not made PCs

APPENDIX C
MILITARY REPRISAL INVESTIGATIVE PLAN AS OF [DATE]

Case Number:	
Investigator:	
Supervisory Investigator:	
Case Summary:	

Complainant(s):			
[Rank]	[Name]	[Service]	[Title]

Subject(s):			
[Rank]	[Name]	[Service]	[Title]

Allegations:		
Alleged Subject	**Allegation**	**Result**
[Name]	REPRISAL/MILITARY	TBD
	Description: [Example: Complainant alleged that RMO gave him an adverse fitness report on March 11, 2013, in reprisal for telling his chain of command that RMO was a toxic leader in 2010.]	

Protected Communication(s):				
Date	**PC**	**To**	**Protected?**	**If No, Why?**
7/24/2012	[Type of PC, e.g., (b)(1)(B) A substantial and specific danger to public health or safety]			
	Description:			

Personnel Action(s):				
Date	**PA**	**By Whom?**	**Covered?**	**If No, Why?**
	Description:			

Documentary Evidence:			
Document Description	**Source**	**Date Requested**	**Date Received**

Witnesses:						
Person			Interview Dates		Transcript Dates	
Name	Duty Position	Type	Scheduled	Completed	Submitted	Received

TDY Location and Dates:					
Description	Personnel	Destination	Departure Date	Return Date	Cost

Investigative Milestones:		
Event	Milestone Date	Date Accomplished
Notification(s) sent		
IP Approval		
Etc.		

APPENDIX D
INTERVIEW READ-IN

Pre-Recording Discussion

We are investigators with the [insert office name] (display credentials and provide business card).

We are conducting an investigation into (summarize the general nature of the allegation(s)).

This is an administrative investigation (not a criminal investigation); we are impartial fact finders and the information you provide may be included in our report of investigation.

Please take a moment to look over this Privacy Act notice (or if you sent the Privacy Notice ahead of time) – do you have any questions?

This interview will be sworn and recorded.

We ask that you not discuss any classified information during the interview -- if there is a need to discuss classified information we can make suitable arrangements to do so at another time.

We caution you that everything you tell us is for the record (we are never off the record – even when the recorder is turned off).

Do you have any questions before we start?

Recorder Is Turned on

Today is DATE. The time is

I am (name of investigator) with the [insert office name]. With me is (name of second investigator).

We are located at (physical location of the interview).

We are conducting this interview as part of our investigation into allegations (summarize the general nature of the allegation(s)).

At this time, I ask you to acknowledge that this interview is being recorded?

Also, acknowledge that I have provided you a copy of the [insert office name] Privacy Act notice.

I will now administer you the oath – please raise your right hand

Do you solemnly swear (affirm) that the testimony you are about to give shall be the truth, the whole truth, and nothing but the truth (so help you God)?

Please state your name, rank/grade and position/duty assignment.

[CONDUCT INTERROGATORY]

Interview Read-Out

Read Out

Is there any additional information that you would like to provide?

Are there other individuals whom we should talk to? Do you have any questions?

If you remember anything else that you believe may be relevant to the investigation, please contact me.

Finally, in order to protect the integrity of the investigation, we ask that you not discuss the matters under investigation or the questions we have asked you during this interview with anyone other than your attorney. This does not apply to or restrict your right to contact an IG or member of Congress.

If anyone asks you about your testimony or the investigation, please inform them that the [insert office name] has asked you not to discuss the matter. If anyone persists in asking you about your testimony or the investigation, or if you feel threatened in any manner because you provided testimony, please contact me.

APPENDIX E

Investigating Officer Checklist
Military Whistleblower Protection Act-10 U.S.C. 1034
XXXXXXX - XXXXXX - **CASE** - XX

Investigator Independence

I attest that:

a. I am outside the immediate chain of command of both the complainant and all subjects or at least one organization higher in the chain of command than the organization of the complainant and all subjects;
b. I am free of personal, financial, or other interests that could influence or be perceived as influencing my handling of this investigation;
c. No one has interfered with or unduly influenced my handling of this investigation; and
d. I have not had a conflict of interest with any witness, the complainant, or any subject during the conduct of this investigation.

IO Name	IO Signature

Investigator Qualifications

Have you received entry-level investigative training?	Yes ☐	No ☐	Date ______	Provider ______
Have you received periodic investigative refresher training?	Yes ☐	No ☐	Date ______ (most recent)	Provider ______

Elements of Reprisal

	YES	NO
1. Making or preparing to make a protected communication, or being perceived as having made a protected communication:		
a. Were all of the protected communications alleged by the complainant identified?	☐	☐
b. Were the dates of the protected communications identified?	☐	☐
c. Were the recipients of the protected communications identified?	☐	☐
d. Were the alleged protection communications analyzed to determine whether they were covered under 10 U.S.C. 1034 and DoDD 7050.06?	☐	☐
2. Unfavorable personnel actions taken or threatened against Complainant, or favorable personnel actions withheld or threatened to be withheld from Complainant:		
a. Were all of the alleged personnel actions identified?	☐	☐
b. Were all of the alleged personnel actions analyzed to determine whether they were covered under 10 U.S.C. 1034 or DoDD 7050.06?	☐	☐
3. Knowledge or perception of responsible official(s) of Complainant's protected communication(s) or preparation of protected communication(s):		
a. Were all of the RMOs identified?	☐	☐
b. Was it determined whether or not each RMO were aware of or perceived that each protected communication took place or was planned?	☐	☐

OIG Investigating Officer Checklist

4. Causation: Did you analyze all factors in determining whether the same personnel action(s) would have been taken, withheld, or threatened absent the protected communication(s):
   a. Reason stated by the RMO for taking, withholding or threatening the action ☐ ☐
   b. Timing between the protected communications and the personnel actions ☐ ☐
   c. RMO's motive for taking, withholding, or threatening the personnel actions, including animosity toward the protected communication ☐ ☐
   d. Disparate treatment of the complainant as compared to other similarly situated individuals ☐ ☐

Analyzing Restriction Allegations N/A YES NO

5. Did you gather and analyze evidence relevant to the question of whether the responsible management official restricted or attempted to restrict a military member or members from making or preparing to make a lawful communication to a member of Congress or an Inspector General? ☐ ☐ ☐

Adherence to Council of the Inspectors General on Integrity and Efficiency Quality Standards YES NO

6. Did you accurately summarize the complaint in the report? ☐ ☐
7. Did you accurately cite and apply the statute or standard that *applied at the time* ☐ ☐
8. Did you identify each underlying allegation or other issues, and were they addressed or referred for handling? N/A YES NO ☐ ☐ ☐
9. Did you prepare an investigative plan? ☐ ☐
10. Did you gather all relevant evidence by:
    a. Interviewing the complainant? ☐ ☐
    b. Interviewing the responsible management official(s)? ☐ ☐
    c. Interviewing relevant witnesses? ☐ ☐
11. For any key witnesses not interviewed, does the report explain why interviews were not conducted? N/A YES NO ☐ ☐ ☐
12. Did you apply the facts to each element of reprisal or to the standard for restriction? ☐ ☐
13. Did you apply the appropriate standard of proof ☐ ☐
14. Does the evidence support the investigative findings? ☐ ☐
15. Did you retain all evidence relied upon in the report and include it with the report for review? ☐ ☐

OIG Investigating Officer Checklist

	N/A	YES	NO
16. If the case has been open over 180 days after receipt of the allegation, have all required notifications been made? USD(P&R), DoD IG, the Secretary of the Military Department concerned, and the complainant?	☐	☐	☐
17. Did the report reach a conclusion for each allegation?		☐	☐
18. If substantiated, did the report recommend appropriate remedy for the complainant?		☐	☐
19. If substantiated, did the report recommend corrective action for the subject(s)?		☐	☐
20. Did the report receive legal sufficiency review?		☐	☐
21. Did the legal review find the report legally sufficient?		☐	☐
22. Does the report include the WRI case number as well as the Service case number?		☐	☐
23. Is the investigative information organized in a logical and easily retrievable manner?		☐	☐

XXXXXXXX-000000-CASE-00 APPENDIX F

WHISTLEBLOWER REPRISAL INVESTIGATION
TITLE/RANK COMPLAINANT'S NAME
AGENCY/SERVICE
LOCATION

I. EXECUTIVE SUMMARY

We conducted this investigation in response to allegations that list RMO information here – name(s) with title/rank, Service/agency, and location did something describe the personnel action(s) here to Complainant's name in reprisal for communicating to whom

We found that concisely summarize the factual findings related to the elements of reprisal.

We substantiated the allegation that RMO name did describe the personnel action in reprisal for Complainant's protected communication(s), in violation of Title 10, United States Code, Section 1034 (10 U.S.C. 1034), "Protected communications; prohibition of retaliatory personnel actions," which is implemented by DoD Directive 7050.06, "Military Whistleblower Protection."

We did not substantiate the allegation that RMO name did not describe the personnel action in reprisal for Complainant's protected communication(s).

We

Comment [Template1]: This first paragraph must include RMO name(s), personnel actions, Complainant's name, and protected communication.

[list RMO information here – name(s) with title and rank, agency/service, and location] [did something]

[describe the personnel action(s) here – did not recommend assignment extension…denied an end-of-tour award…gave an unfavorable noncommissioned officer evaluation report…] to [complainant's name]
in reprisal for communicating to his command's information systems security manager…to his command IG…).

Comment [Template2]: For substantiated allegations state…

Comment [Template3]: For allegations not substantiated, state . . .

Comment [Template4]: If there are multiple RMOs having different findings, summarize them separately as in the paragraph above; however, if they collectively took the actions, summarize them together.

Comment [Template5]: State what you recommended and to whom; in cases where you do not make any recommendations, state: We did not make any recommendations in this matter.

II. BACKGROUND

Complainant …

III. SCOPE

This investigation covered the period from

IV. STATUTORY AUTHORITY

The Department of Defense Inspector General (DoD) IG conducted this whistleblower reprisal investigation pursuant to Title 10, United States Code, Section 1034 (10 U.S.C. 1034), "Protected communications; prohibition of retaliatory personnel actions," which is implemented by DoD Directive 7050.06, "Military Whistleblower Protection."

V. FINDINGS OF FACT

Heading

Set subheadings in at .5. DO NOT UNDERLINE!

Heading

Heading

VI. ANALYSIS

The elements of reprisal are protected communication, knowledge of the protected communication on the part of the responsible management official; a personnel action taken, threatened, or withheld; and a causal connection between the protected communication and the personnel action. The causal connection is resolved by answering the question in paragraph D, below. If the evidence does not establish that the personnel action would have been taken, threatened, or withheld even absent the protected communication, then the complaint is substantiated. Conversely, if the evidence establishes that it would have been taken, threatened, or withheld absent the protected communication, then the complaint is not substantiated. Below, we analyze each of the elements.

A. Did Complainant make or prepare to make a protected communication , or was Complainant perceived as having made or prepared to make a protected communication?

We determined that Complainant made number protected communications under 10 U.S.C. 1034 and number communications were not protected.

Comment [Template6]: This section can be as short as one paragraph. *The detailed chronological telling of the facts involved in the investigation should be in the "FINDINGS OF FACT" section. **Other key individuals involved in the investigation should be identified in the "FINDINGS OF FACT" section as they come into the story chronologically.

Comment [Template7]: This section should provide the reader information about the organizations, command relationships, and Complainant and management officials involved in the matter under investigation. Give a brief overview of events that led to the protected communication and personnel action. It may also be used to provide a very brief chronology or synopsis of key events ***leading up to*** the matters under investigation but generally not the matters ***directly*** under investigation. Do not include detailed narratives of the facts of the case that are presented in the Findings of Fact section of the report.

Comment [Template8]: This section should describe the scope of the investigation in summary terms, leading with a statement of the ***timeframe*** addressed by the investigation, followed by ***key*** witnesses interviewed and ***crucial*** documents reviewed. Do not list every witness and every type of document. Include subject matter experts if their testimony was crucial to the outcome of the investigation.

Comment [Template9]: THIS BOILERPLATE LANGUAGE SHOULD NOT CHANGE.

Comment [Template10]: This section is a chronological telling of ONLY the RELEVANT facts involved in the story we've found in the investigation. Don't discuss the facts in terms of protected communications, personnel actions, RMO knowledge, stated reason, RMO motive, animus, and disparate treatment.
Do not, for example, find that a visit to the IG is a protected communication or an unfavorable OER is a personnel action, or that an email to an RMO gave them knowledge of a protected communication etc. In the "ANALYSIS" section, we will answer the questions related to the elements of reprisal using the facts established in this section.

Comment [Template11]: Many paragraphs in the section will start with something like "On DATE, Complainant…." Use transition words and phrases for readability (ex: Following that, … After that, … Concurrently, ….)

Comment [Template12]: Tell what happened, not what the testimony was about what happened. For facts not in dispute, state, for example, "Complainant told RMO during a meeting on September 11 that she inventoried the stock and found a significant discrepancy between the invoices and stock on hand," instead of "Complainant testified…. RMO testified…, etc." Refer specifically to testimony or other evidence only where there are factual disputes in the testimony and resolve those discrepancies here in the factual ...

Comment [Template13]: Set subheadings in at .5. DO NOT UNDERLINE

Thus, a preponderance of the evidence established that Complainant

B. Was an unfavorable personnel action taken or threatened against Complainant, or was a favorable personnel action withheld or threatened to be withheld from Complainant?

We determined that Complainant was or was not the subject of a personnel action as defined by 10 U.S.C. 1034.

Alleged personnel action #1

Alleged personnel action #2

Thus, a preponderance of the evidence established that Complainant

C. Did the responsible management official(s) have knowledge of Complainant's protected communication(s) or perceive Complainant as making or preparing protected communication(s)?

We determined that RMO name knew and second RMO name knew that Complainant had communicated with who and third RMO's name had no knowledge of any protected communications.

Thus, a preponderance of the evidence established that RMO name

D. Would the same personnel action(s) have been taken, withheld, or threatened absent the protected communication(s)? [Include D only if questions A-C are all answered in the affirmative.]

We determined that RMO name would/would not have taken the personnel actions against the Complainant absent his/her protected communications.

Comment [Template14]: Use a short paragraph for each alleged protected communication that synthesizes information already in the "FINDINGS OF FACT." Do not introduce new facts. This is merely listing each alleged protected communication and showing your determination that it either is or is not in fact a protected communication and why. **These should not begin** with "We found," or "So-and-so stated." They should end with a statement saying that an alleged protected communication is or is not protected under 10 U.S.C. 1034 and why.

Comment [Template15]: When the investigation covers **only one** protected communication, the first paragraph should synthesize the facts related to the protected communication and determine whether or not it is protected.

When the investigation covers **more than one** protected communication, the first paragraph should summarize the different protected communications (not the facts for each protected communication) and serve as a topic paragraph for the section. Then s ...

Comment [Template16]: Close the section with a sentence or paragraph that begins "Thus, a preponderance of the evidence established that Complainant. . ."

Comment [Template17]: State personnel action here if there is only one.

Comment [Template18]: The follow-on sentences/paragraphs should present the analysis of whether the facts as stated above constitute a personnel action. **These should not begin** with "We found," or "So and so stated." Do not introduce new facts. End with a statement saying that the action ...

Comment [Template19]: When the investigation covers only one personnel action, this paragraph should synthesize the facts related to the personnel action and determine whether or not it is a personnel action under the statute. ...

Comment [Template20]: Close the section with a sentence or paragraph that begins, "Thus, a preponderance of the evidence established that Complainant . . ."

Comment [Template21]: The follow-on sentences/paragraphs should synthesize the facts related to knowledge and determine whether or not the evidence established that the RMOs had knowledge. **These should not begin with** "We found," or "So and so stated."

Comment [Template22]: When the investigation covers only one RMO and one protected communication, the paragraph should summarize the relevant facts. When the investigation covers more than one RMO or more than one protected communication, the very first ...

Comment [Template23]: To make this determination, for each action taken, we analyze the following factors:
the strength of the evidence in support of the stated reason for the personnel action; ...

RMO's name ***stated reasons for*** *personnel action*

Timing between protected communication and personnel action

RMO's name ***motive to reprise***

Disparate treatment of Complainant

Thus, a preponderance of the evidence established that RMO name would/would not …

VI. DISCUSSION

VII. CONCLUSION(S)

We conclude, by a preponderance of the evidence, that:

RMO name did/did not (personnel action) Complainant in reprisal for protected communication.

Second RMO name did/did not (personnel action) Complainant in reprisal for protected communication.

Third RMO name did/did not (personnel action) Complainant in reprisal for protected communication.

VIII. RECOMMENDATION(S)

We make no recommendations in this matter.

We recommend that the Secretary of the Military Service/Agency direct Military Service/Agency officials to:

Insert appropriate relief to make Complainant whole.

Take appropriate corrective action against RMO name

Comment [Template24]: Consider and analyze all of the following factors that are applicable to the facts and evidence. The follow-on sentences/paragraphs should present the synthesized findings of fact—what happened, based on the evidence. **These should not begin** with "We found," or "So and so stated."

Comment [Template25]: •
- •Each RMO's stated reason(s) for the personnel action(s)
- •Timing between the protected communication(s) and personnel action(s)
- •Motive on the part of the RMO(s) to reprise, including any animosity expressed by the RMO(s) regarding the protected communications
- •Disparate treatment of Complainant as compared to other similarly situated individuals who did not make protected communications

Comment [Template26]: Close the section with a sentence or paragraph that begins, "Thus, a preponderance of the evidence established that [RMO's name] would/would not…."

Comment [Template27]: Synthesize the analysis above **in one or two paragraphs**, explaining how we arrived at our conclusions. For example: "Based on a preponderance of the evidence, we conclude that [RMO name] issued an adverse OPR in reprisal for Complainant's protected communication to the IG. The evidence shows that Complainant's protected communication resulted in an investigation that substantiated misconduct by the RMO, who knew Complainant made the protected communication. [RMO name] told his XO and others that he was upset that Complainant went outside of the chain of command. Finally, the evidence shows that Complainant had received glowing OPR's prior to his protected communication, etc."

Comment [Template28]: When not substantiated.

Comment [Template29]: When substantiated, use the following . . .

XXXXXXXX-000000-CASE-00

WHISTLEBLOWER RESTRICTION INVESTIGATION
TITLE/RANK COMPLAINANT'S NAME
AGENCY/SERVICE
LOCATION

APPENDIX G

I. EXECUTIVE SUMMARY

We conducted this investigation in response to allegations that [list RMO information here – name(s) with title and rank, agency/service, and location] restricted [or attempted to restrict] [complainant's name] from making or preparing to make a lawful communication to communicating with a member of Congress or an Inspector General. This first paragraph must include RMO name(s) and Complainant's name.

We found that…[concisely summarize the factual findings related to the alleged restriction. For example: We found that [RMO's name] told complainant via email on [Date] that if she contacted the IG again there would be dire consequences.].

For substantiated allegations, state: We conclude that [RMO's name] did [describe the restriction] in violation of Title 10, United States Code, Section 1034 (10 U.S.C. 1034), "Protected communications; prohibition of retaliatory personnel actions," which is implemented by DoD Directive 7050.06, "Military Whistleblower Protection." For allegations we did not substantiate, state: We conclude that [RMO's name] did not [describe the restriction] in violation of Title 10, United States Code, Section 1034 (10 U.S.C. 1034), "Protected communications; prohibition of retaliatory personnel actions," which is implemented by DoD Directive 7050.06, "Military Whistleblower Protection."

If there are multiple RMOs having different findings, summarize them separately as in the paragraph above; however, if they collectively took the actions, summarize them together.

State what you recommended and to whom; in cases where you do not make any recommendations, state: We did not make any recommendations in this matter.

Insert case number here

II. BACKGROUND

This section should provide the reader information about the organizations, command relationships, and key individuals involved in the investigation. Give a brief overview of events that led to the protected communication and personnel action. It may also be used to provide a very brief chronology or synopsis of key events ***leading up to*** the matters under investigation but generally not the matters ***directly*** under investigation. Do not include detailed narratives of the facts of the case that are presented in the Findings of Fact section of the report.

III. SCOPE

This section should describe the scope of the investigation in summary terms, leading with a statement of the ***timeframe*** addressed by the investigation, followed by ***key*** witnesses interviewed and ***crucial*** documents reviewed. Do not list every witness and every type of document. Include subject matter experts if their testimony was crucial to the outcome of the investigation.

IV. STATUTORY AUTHORITY

This boilerplate statutory language should not change:

The [name of office conducting investigation] conducted this whistleblower restriction investigation pursuant to Title 10, United States Code, Section 1034 (10 U.S.C. 1034), "Protected communications; prohibition of retaliatory personnel actions," which is implemented by DoD Directive 7050.06, "Military Whistleblower Protection."

V. FINDINGS OF FACT

We found that ….

VI. ANALYSIS

Did the responsible management official (RMO) restrict or attempt to restrict Complainant from making or preparing to make a lawful communication to a member of Congress or an Inspector General?

We determined that the responsible management official restricted/did not restrict Complainant….

[Consider and analyze all of the evidence relating to the RMO's restriction or attempt to restrict the Complainant's communication with a member of Congress or an Inspector General.]

VII. DISCUSSION

Insert case number here

VI. CONCLUSION(S)

We conclude:

[RMO's name] [did/did not restrict] Complainant in violation of 10 U.S.C. 1034.

VII. RECOMMENDATION(S)

When not substantiated:

We make no recommendations in this matter.

OR, when substantiated:

We recommend that the [Secretary of the Military Service/Agency] direct [Military Service/Agency] officials to:

[Take appropriate corrective action against RMO(s).]

Service/Agency letterhead

APPENDIX H

[Rank Abbreviation Full Name, Service abbreviation] [Case Number]
[Street Address]
[City, State Zip]
[Email address]

Dear [Rank last name]:

This letter is to update you on our investigation into the complaint you filed under Title 10, United States Code, Section 1034, "Protected communications; prohibition of retaliatory personnel actions," as implemented by DoD Directive 7050.06, "Military Whistleblower Protection."

Section 1034(e)(3) requires that we notify you and the Secretary of Defense if we are unable to complete the report of investigation within the 180-day statutory timeframe and that we tell you when we expect to complete the investigation. Further, under paragraph 5.1.6 of the DoD Directive, we are also required to notify you of the reason for the delay.

Over 180 days have passed since you filed this complaint on [enter date]. [Enter brief explanation of the reason for the delay.] We anticipate that the investigation will be completed within the next 90 days.

Please contact [Mr./Ms. Investigator or Supervisory Investigator name], [investigator title], at [phone number] or DSN [number] or by email at [enter Investigator or Supervisory Investigator email] if you have any questions.

Sincerely,

[SI Full Name]
Supervisory Investigator
Whistleblower Reprisal Investigations

cc:
Director, Enterprise Services
Office of the Under Secretary of Defense for Personnel and Readiness
[Service Secretary of the military department concerned]
DoD IG, Whistleblower Reprisal Investigations

Service/Agency letterhead
D R A F T

APPENDIX I

[Rank Abbreviation Full Name, Service abbreviation] [Case Number]
[Street Address]
[City, State Zip]
[Email address]

Dear [Rank last name]:

We have completed an investigation into your complaint of reprisal under Title 10, United States Code, Section 1034 (10 U.S.C. 1034), "Protected communications; prohibition of retaliatory personnel actions," implemented by DoD Directive 7050.06, "Military Whistleblower Protection."

Your complaint (was or was not) substantiated. Enclosed is a copy of the report of investigation, redacted to exclude information exempt from release under the Freedom of Information and Privacy Acts.

Under 10 U.S.C. 1034, you may request review of the matter by the [enter appropriate Board name] (board abbreviation). Should you wish to do so, complete and mail the enclosed application (DD 149) to the [Service] address listed on the reverse of the form.

Should you have any questions, please contact [Mr./Ms. Investigator or Supervisory Investigator name], [investigator title], at [phone number] , DSN [number], or email at [email address].

Sincerely,

Enclosures:
As stated

cc:
OUSD P&R Chief of Staff
DoD OIG WRI
[Board abbreviation]

INDEX

L

M

N

O

P

Q

R

S

T

U

V

W